How To Repair and Maintain **American V-Twin Motorcycles**

How To Repair and Maintain **American V-Twin Motorcycles**

Sara Liberte
Photography by Chaz Palla

MOTORBOOKS

I'd like to dedicate this book to Mark L'heurux for inspiring me to combine my two passions: motorcycles and photography. Ride in peace, Mark. I wish I could thank you for all the knowledge you shared with me.

First published in 2006 by Motorbooks, an imprint of MBI Publishing Company, Galtier Plaza, Suite 200, 380 Jackson Street, St. Paul, MN 55101-3885 USA

MBI Publishing Company titles are also available at discounts in bulk quantity for industrial or sales-promotional use. For details write to Special Sales Manager at MBI Publishing Company, Galtier Plaza, Suite 200, 380 Jackson Street, St. Paul, MN 55101-3885 USA

ISBN-13: 978-0-7603-2354-0
ISBN-10: 0-7603-2354-2

On the front cover, main: Author Sara Liberte and a custom Rev Tech softail chopper she built at her shop, North Hills Cycle.

Inset: When replacing your primary cover, always use a new gasket. They're inexpensive and will save you loads of hassle down the road.

On the back cover: Having a bike lift and a clean, organized workspace will make work easier and encourage you to spend more time in your garage getting to know your motorcycle.

Editor: Peter Schletty
Designer: Chris Fayers

Printed in China

CONTENTS

PREFACE

Being a custom motorcycle shop owner has forced me to see the way people maintain their bikes. Some are on top of the game, but most don't understand or have the direction to do what they should to maintain their motorcycles.

I believe servicing your own bike is a part of being a motorcyclist. I wrote this book to get riders more familiar with their motorcycles and to introduce the service manual (which I believe every bike owner should have on hand) to riders.

This book covers everything from an explanation of the V-Twin engine and how it works to torque specs on a wheel. Each chapter walks you through the very basics of maintaining and servicing your own bike. This book is not intended to replace the service manual but to work as an encouraging tool to get you to pick up some wrenches and take on the responsibility of maintaining your motorcycle.

The motorcycle is an extension of the body. Treat it the way you treat yourself and your riding time will be that much more enjoyable. You must remember that safety should always be top bill when doing any service work on your motorcycle. Wear eye protection when needed and use caution with any power tools.

ACKNOWLEDGMENTS

First and foremost, I want to thank my parents, Dave and Diane, for all the encouragement and love they gave me and continue to give today. I also must thank my brother Craig and sister Karen for reminding me that anything cool happened before I was born; my boyfriend Ron Tonetti (R.T.) for always being by my side and for sharing all of his knowledge with me; my nephew Anthony and niece Rachel for the innocence and joy they share; and Brian for building me the greatest workspace.

Thank you to the two teachers in my life who taught me lessons I use every day in my work: Christine O'Brien and Linda White. Thanks to Eric Neszpaul for art direction like no one else could deliver; Chaz Palla for photography the way I like it; and Dave Nichols, JJ Handfield, Mike Seate, Darwin Holmstrom, and Ernie Lopez for not treating me like "just a girl"; and Chris Callen for being my "brother." Gratitude to Bel-Ray Oils, Performance Machine, Tech Starters, CruzTOOLS, Ferodo TP, and S&S Cycle.

I also have to thank Goth Girl, Joann Bortels, Sam Morgan Storm, and the American Motor Drome gang for being the coil and kicking some voltage my way to make me spark again. I love you all.

INTRODUCTION:
About me, by Sara Liberte

Every day men and women are doing thousands of demanding tasks on their own: running a home and/or business, raising children, holding down a job, and maintaining their bodies. Why not add the maintenance of their motorcycle to the list? People depend on themselves to get lots of things done, and keeping their motorcycle in order should be one of them.

My work began in 1994 in Boston as a sophomore attending Montserratt College of Art. I've always had a fascination for metal and all things mechanical. Growing up in a family-owned steel business, I found myself enticed by these hard, heavy objects. My passion soon grew to things that made power and contained beauty. My dad was heavy into cars, and going to car shows at an early age got me hooked.

In my teen years I started to become interested in motorcycles, specifically American-made V-Twin bikes. The shape of the V-Twin engine was gorgeous. I became obsessed with motorcycles, the fact that man designed this machine to fit himself perfectly. Shift with your feet, throttle with your hands, you control the power, you are the bike. I connected with that.

Growing up, my generation of young women believed that we would marry and raise a family, have dinner waiting on the table for our husbands, and life would be great. That dream I cherished and held onto throughout my childhood and teen years. Then college came and I soon began to realize that dream was never going to happen, not in the world I was living in during the early 1990s. I found out I needed independence, to make my own path and provide for myself.

In this struggle with reality I turned to what gave me strength in my childhood: metal, power, and machines. Motorcycles became my new passion of machines. These objects were strong and independent. These objects were solid, not flimsy. They were so tough, they reeked of independence.

During my study in art school I began photographing images of the female body, so delicate, curvy, soft, and warm. While working in the darkroom I discovered a connection between my images of delicate females and the tough, hard images of engines and motorcycle components. Not only was the connection internal in displaying the independence of woman and machine, but visual through texture, shape, and movement.

The way to express my desire to be strong and survive on my own was in these images—showing how woman could accept life and its challenges while providing for herself. The work became a mission: To express that women all over were, in fact, strong and capable of existence without the help of someone else.

One consistency in women's position in society has been the stereotype of the weaker sex, a sex object, or a selling point in the automotive and commercial industry. While we may embody some of those qualities, women are also strong, motivated, tough, and consistent. Women never stop. We are machines.

My work explains this connection. Images of engines, machines, and motorcycles fused with soft, curvy females. The two have become one for me. On the outside we are beautiful, warm, soft, and delicate. Inside we are strong, tough as metal, and hard, like engines enduring thousands of miles throughout the journey of life.

As my photography career grew I met my boyfriend, Ron Tonetti, in Laconia, New Hampshire, during bike week. Photographing the many bikes he's built and painted, Ron and I started a relationship and soon a business. Together we run RT's North Hills Cycle Inc. We build and paint custom bikes.

I'm involved in every aspect of the business, from design to sheet-metal fabrication to paint and the basic service work. I'm also the lucky girl who runs the office, handles the accounting, and manages parts and service. I'm lucky in that I have a job that I love, a job where I can use my imagination to create not only rolling sculptures but photographic art, where my vision can carry through my career and hopefully inspire people to be strong, independent, and want to be in control of their own motorcycle. The most "in control" you can feel while riding your bike is knowing the working condition of your bike firsthand. This is what everyone who rides should feel: Total control of your machine.

Some people might not yet have a bike. I'd like to stress the importance of the Motorcycle Safety Foundation (MSF) course, which is available in every state. The easiest way to get information is by checking out their website at www.msf-usa.org. This course is the place to start if you are interested in learning to ride. Even if you ride now and never took the course, the lessons you will learn from it will stay with you and give you an advantage on the street. I attended it back in Massachusetts and I don't care what your riding level skill is, you will learn something from this course. So please, consider the Motorcycle Safety Foundation Rider Course.

Sara Liberte and her boyfriend R.T. (center) with friends.

CHAPTER 1
KNOW YOUR RIDE

Your first ride was more than likely on the back of someone else's bike. The thrill of the wind in your hair, the power of the bike, the sound of the exhaust, and the smells of the road probably had you hooked in the first eighth of a mile. The excitement had you starving for more riding time and the idea of having to wait for someone to take you for a ride just wasn't going to satisfy your appetite.

You couldn't sit still, longed to be free and out on the road again, to see the world up close becoming part of the environment, not just an onlooker. Saving up all your money you go ahead and purchase your own bike. The first ride on that bike put you in total control of the machine. The power at your fingertips made you feel independent, in command, and free. You think nothing can top that feeling, that just hopping on and going for a blast is utopia.

I used to think that way until I learned how to wrench on my own ride. Spinning wrenches on your own bike leaves you with completeness and the satisfaction of knowing firsthand that your bike is in top running condition. This pride and independence takes the next ride to another level. You're on top, and you're in total control.

My first desire to turn wrenches started in high school. I had just turned sixteen and my dad hooked me up with a sweet 1966 Mustang hardtop. I thought nothing would top the feeling I got cruising around town in that car. My dad would bring me to car shows and I loved driving my Mustang into the car corrals.

I'd get lots of people asking questions about what was under the hood. "An engine, of course," I'd say. I'd get lots of laughs, but guys really wanted to know what was powering my ride.

I wanted to know, too. What was making that car burn tire when I stomped on the gas pedal? I began paying attention to the way the car was running and the response of the throttle, looking under the hood, cleaning the engine up.

I told my dad the car was feeling sluggish and we had to figure out why. He was a mechanic, and after some

A good quality leather jacket, like this Vanson, will not only protect you from the elements, it will also protect your body from "road rash" in the event of an accident.

Depending on what state you live in, you might be required to wear a DOT-approved helmet. In any case, helmet, gloves, and eye protection should be part of your riding gear. Be sure to inspect your riding gear every once in a while to make sure everything is in good shape.

When picking out a pair of riding boots, make sure your ankle will be covered for protection and support. Make sure you pick a boot that is comfortable as well—you'll be flexing your foot when shifting and applying the brake.

troubleshooting together we decided to rebuild the carb. He let me help out and turn a few wrenches. When I fired up the car and took it out for a spin, that feeling I thought I couldn't top was surpassed when the Mustang ran like a champ again. Knowing I had a hand in rebuilding the carb, making the car run so good, made the ride so much more exciting.

I opened my bike shop back in April of 1999 when R.T. and I purchased an established motorcycle business from a friend. When we first opened I ran the whole deal, selling parts and troubleshooting bikes while Ron worked at an auto parts store to keep a steady income rolling in for us. Soon after opening the shop we started to get busy and we

Chaps aren't necessary riding gear, but they come in handy on cold nights and long trips. Besides keeping you warm, they will protect your legs in the unfortunate case of an accident.

started doing full services so as not to lose that potential paint-job client or tire sale. For two years I changed tires by hand with a bead-breaker and tire spoons. I'm so glad my shop now has a tire machine.

The paint jobs soon started to come in and we were headed in the right direction. As the shop grew busier my position as owner had to keep changing. Not only parts manager, I was now service manager and part-time mechanic, as well as designer and custom paint artist. Let's not forget I was still doing freelance photography all along and maintaining a staff position with the *Cycle Source* magazine.

Oil changes were easy and something I could bang out quick while Ron had an engine or paint job to work on. My mechanical duties started to go beyond oil changes, however, and soon I was tearing down top ends. I vowed to remain a left-hand wrench since putting things back together required too much concentration and referencing torque specs in the dozens of shop manuals we had for all the different models of bikes.

It didn't take long for the custom builds and paint jobs to start coming in once people saw our quality of work. Ron and I are a great team. I will design the sheet metal, the paint job, and the artwork for the customer while Ron works his magic with the spray gun.

As I began gaining knowledge about the bikes and the joy of working on them, I decided it was time to start maintaining my own bike instead of leaving that job up to Ron. I started with fluid changes and, when the problem

presented itself, gasket changes, belt tension adjustment, and tire changes (still by hand).

I learned about preventative maintenance as well. Every time I would get on my bike to go for a ride I would check things over, my tire pressure, my electrical components, make sure my brake lights, my turn signals, and my horn were working. I'd never forgive myself if something was to happen on the road and it was discovered that I had a turn signal out. For me, I couldn't live with knowing I could have prevented an accident if I had just taken a few seconds to look my bike over before I left for my ride.

I immediately began to feel more confident riding my bike after doing the basic services myself. I knew firsthand the working condition of my bike and nothing made me feel more in control than that.

As the shop got busier I found myself with less and less riding time. I had no need to ride to work, since we live at our shop. I couldn't even blow off a day from work to go riding because that wouldn't pay the bills or look good to our customers. Since my saddle time was few and far between, I needed a way to connect to my bike. Wrenching was my connection. It soon became my favorite connection.

WEARING THE PROPER RIDING GEAR

Preparing yourself with the proper riding gear is the first step to maintaining yourself and your bike: boots, gloves, eye protection, leather jacket, and helmet. You can be the world's greatest rider but that doesn't stand up against the other guy

You can see that this hardtail frame has no rear suspension. You can't beat the look of a hardtail, but you also can't beat the riding comfort of a bike equipped with rear suspension.

On this stock Softail chassis you can see the triangle shape of the swingarm creating the look of a hardtail while keeping the shocks underneath the frame and out of view.

Above left: Here is an exposed spring-type shock found on XLs and Dyna chassis. Checking out the suspension is a quick way to identify what model of bike you're looking at. Above right: Normally hidden by saddlebags, the FL chassis use a canister-style shock, usually air-filled as shown here. These shocks work the same as the exposed spring-style shock.

on the road who "just didn't see you." So be smart and be safe. You are responsible for yourself and you must do all you can to ensure your well-being with your bike and body. Don't leave your destiny up in the air.

Day after day I will get people rolling into the shop on their bikes wearing shorts, T-shirts, and sandals. Yes, sandals. Imagine how that big toe is going to feel if you slip off your foot peg and slam your toe into the pavement cruising at 45 miles per hour. Ouch! Please wear full-covered shoes, preferably boots, that will support and protect your toes and ankles. Yeah, OK, I know it's hot and you're sweating, but come on! You have to be smart.

Have you ever seen what road rash looks like? It's not pretty and the pain is worse than it looks! Worse yet is how it's treated at the hospital, with wire brushes to clean it out. Need I say more? Road rash won't win you any beauty contests, that's for sure. A simple leather jacket is a great defense against road rash.

You see, the whole basis of this book is to prepare you to be ready for the road, to do all you can to ensure a safe, fun, and secure ride by properly maintaining your motorcycle. Before we maintain our bikes we have to maintain ourselves. Please, invest in proper riding gear.

A great pair of riding glasses will keep your eyes safe from debris and tears leaving you with full vision so you can see where you're going, and that's a good thing, isn't it? Being able to see clearly is important especially on a motorcycle. Have you ever been blinded by the sun while driving your car? It's impossible to see anything. You start to swerve and slow down to a crawl because you can't see what may be coming your way. Now you're traveling so slow that the car coming up behind you can't see either because the sun is blinding them and they have no idea how slow you are going. Can you see how this is a recipe for disaster? Imagine dealing with that loss of vision on your bike.

Above left: A front end with 39-mm forks is very common. The front end consists of the fork tubes, lower sliders, and internal springs. A dampener tube connects the fork tubes to the sliders allowing suspension movement. Above right: This springer front end, named for the obvious visible springs, consists of a rigid mounted leg and a spring leg connected by rockers to which the wheel is mounted. Later springer front ends incorporate a shock absorber where earlier models did not.

In my opinion, a helmet is a vital piece of riding gear. Many people disagree on this issue, and since it's a free country some states will let you choose whether to wear one or not. Regardless of what I or anyone else says, it does come down to your choice. A DOT-approved helmet will protect in ways I don't think I need to get into. We all know the protection a helmet can provide.

My instructor in the Motorcycle Safety Foundation course saw me ride into the class with one of those fake beanie helmets on my head. My instructor then asked me if I had a $40 brain. I didn't have a response.

He asked, "What is your brain worth? How much education have you had?"

At the time I was in my second year of college, so I answered, "High school and a little college."

"Tuition isn't cheap, is it?" he asked. I agreed.

He then said, "So why not wear a helmet that protects your investment?"

Needless to say, I now wear a DOT helmet when I ride my motorcycle.

The last important thing to remember is a good pair of gloves. Gloves are something you should always ride with. If something were to happen and you had to lay your bike down, the first thing to hit the ground due to your first reaction will be your hands. When falling, initial human instinct is to put our hands out in front of us to keep ourselves safe. So keep those hands one step ahead of the game and keep 'em covered. Riding gloves will also give you better grip on your handlebars, and control is a top priority. Make sure to get a pair of riding gloves that fit properly. Not too loose, not too tight.

This information is not meant to scare you; it's to help you build a better rider in yourself. The best way to be a better rider is to be smart, and to be smart you must know your bike as well as yourself and maintain them both properly. Trust me, your rides will be much more enjoyable knowing that you are prepared and your motorcycle is as well.

Above left: This Wide Glide front has larger-diameter 41-mm fork tubes spaced farther apart than the 39-mm narrow glide. Internally, the suspension works the same with all the same parts. Above right: At quick glance you can tell by this massive front end that you're looking at an FL-style chassis. Internally the suspension works the same as a narrow glide, but external dimensions and styling are different. Most obvious are the "fork tins," which hide the fork tubes and give the bike a massive look.

Hidden under the frame, Softail shocks are mounted horizontally and run front to back. The shocks are located under the transmission. Inside, the shocks consist of a large-diameter, short-length stiff spring wrapped around a hydraulic dampener.

This V-Rod uses the exposed-style shock on its unique chassis.

HOW TO TELL CHASSIS APART

In order to maintain your bike you have to know your bike's "make" or manufacturer (i.e., Harley or Honda). Which "model" you have (i.e., Softail or Dyna). And most important, know your model year. This information will be needed when you go to the parts counter to buy parts for your bike.

There are a few different types of chassis available. This book is based around the American V-Twin models, Harley-Davidsons, and customs. But you can apply most of what I'm saying to any bike. All bikes have service manuals, and all the information you need will be in the manual. So if you don't have an American bike you don't have to stop reading.

Harley, for example, sells a Softail chassis, a Dyna chassis, an FLH chassis, the Sportster chassis, and an FXR chassis. The easiest way to tell what type of chassis you're looking at is by looking at the suspension. If you can see the shock from the swingarm to the fender strut then you're looking at a Sportster, Dyna, or FXR. If you can't see a shock and the frame continues straight down to the axle of the frame, then you're

looking at a hardtail, which has no suspension in the rear. The only suspension is in the front end. (A very rough ride if you live in a landscape, like I do, in western Pennsylvania. These chassis are better suited for flat landscapes and smooth roads.)

If you can see what appears to be a triangle swingarm on the end of the bike's frame that gives the illusion of a hardtail frame, you're looking at a softail chassis. The shocks are mounted under the bike and are not easily viewable. The softail chassis was designed to keep the clean smooth lines of the hardtail but to make the ride more enjoyable on your kidneys and internal organs with a rear suspension. FLH models and Road Kings have an exposed shock, usually a canister-style shock that's typically air-filled. These are normally hidden by the hard saddlebags.

The most unique chassis and my personal favorite is the FXR. This chassis has an exposed shock, but where the shock mounts up at the fender strut you will find a triangle section in the frame near the seat. This bike is rubber mounted, as are the Dyna and 5-speed FL chassis, certain newer Twin-Cam models, as well as newer Sportsters. A rubber-mounted bike has rubber isolators mounting the engine to the frame. A rubber-mounted bike is generally a smoother ride, but it's different in the sense that you won't feel that "Harley shake" through your fingers into your body and through your feet into your legs.

So that's a quick breakdown of how to determine the chassis of your bike. Foreign bikes have similar looking chassis, but you'll find some have different final drives. Some use a shaft drive where there will be no final chain or belt. Otherwise, the basics of the frame stay the same.

VIN NUMBERS

Another way to identify the chassis is the VIN number. The VIN number is always located in two places: On the engine case and (on 1970 and later models) the frame tag. Every manufacturer is different, and many will hide VIN numbers on other parts of the motorcycle as a security measure. But every motorcycle will have a VIN number etched on the

All motorcycles manufactured after 1970 (unless custom built) will have a tag or decal on the frame. Here you can find important information like the Vehicle Identification Number (VIN), weight of the bike, maximum load capacity, and tire info.

The VIN is also stamped on the engine case pictured here. On earlier models (pre-1970), this is often the only place to find the VIN. Stars indicate the beginning and end of the engine VIN.

engine and frame. Stars note the beginning and end of the VIN number stamped on the engine case. On older models, pre-1970, the VIN number was only stamped on the engine case where the two cylinders meet.

Like an automobile, the number sequence is broken down by digit. A chart explaining each digit will be listed in your service manual. It defines model, year, engine displacement, country or plant of manufacture, and sequential production number. Your VIN number is also a security device, making it easy to identify a bike that may have been stolen.

Take the time to familiarize yourself with your VIN number and reference to your service manual what each digit represents. You'll soon be able to identify a bike by looking at the VIN numbers.

FAMILIARIZE YOURSELF WITH IMPORTANT FEATURES OF YOUR BIKE

There are certain features of your bike you should know off the top of your head. This information will come in handy when ordering parts to ensure you get the correct part for your model bike. They include:
The year of your bike
The make and model of your bike
Tire sizes
Wheel sizes
Fuel tank capacity
Brake pad part number
Headlight style (sealed beam or H4 bulb)
Engine style and size
Final drive (belt or chain)
Primary drive (belt or chain)
Fluid capacity

PARTS ORDERING

I can't tell you how many people come in to my shop and ask for an oil filter. Certain filters fit certain bikes, so I'll ask the customer their make, model, and year. They'll usually just tell me "It's a Harley." That doesn't cut it.

Certain parts fit certain bikes for a reason. The reason it's important is because parts will change for the same model within model years. For instance, an oil filter for a 2002 Twin Cam Softail will not work for a 1998 Evo Softail. Oil filters for the Twin Cam engine use a 10-micron filtration system. If you put a Twin Cam oil filter on an Evo engine it will literally blow oil everywhere because the 10-micron filter causes Evo engines to collect excessive oil in the crankcase at the bottom of the engine.

Knowing exactly what you ride is extremely important for correct parts ordering. It can prevent something as simple as using the wrong oil filter and causing a major mess or worse! It's also important for dress-up items you might want to buy for your bike. Just like with the hard parts, dress-up accessories will only fit certain models and years. You might want to jot down your make, model, and year somewhere safe so you can access it easily if you have a bad memory like I do.

It's also important to buy quality parts and accessories. Sure, you'll find a few different variations of the same part with a noticeable price difference. But believe me, you won't be getting a bargain if you choose the lesser-quality part. Do some research and check around to see what other people recommend. Magazines often test products, and your local mechanic will surely have a recommendation or two. We see the results of poor quality parts every day. The more information you have on hand at the parts counter, the more you will increase your odds of getting exactly what you need.

So many older bikes have been wrenched on or put together by mechanics with, shall we say, lack of mechanical knowledge. If you bought an older bike that has a hodgepodge of parts assembled to create a rolling chassis, you're in for hell at the parts counter. Your title may say you bought a 1977 FX bike, but your front end or transmission, or even engine, may not be stock. This gets confusing when ordering. For example, let's say your bike should have come with a single brake setup on the front end but the bike you purchased has a dual-disc front end. If you want to replace your lower legs and order a front end for your 1977 FX, you won't have what you need to accommodate the dual disc.

If you own an older mix-and-match bike, do yourself a favor and find out exactly what parts are on the bike you have. A very common modification people do to their bikes is to change the fuel tank and often the location of the dash equipment. This can cause problems when trying to re-order a speedometer cable. Your best bet is to bring the part you want to replace to the parts salesperson and let them set you up with a new one.

HOW TO USE YOUR SERVICE MANUAL

So you're ready to take on the task of servicing your own bike. First you must buy a service manual for your model of bike. Not the owner's manual that comes with the bike, but a service manual. This is the book that all professional mechanics use. We use these books daily in my shop. Service manuals are the encyclopedias of wrenching and they're available at any bike shop, dealer, or aftermarket supplier. All the information you will need to wrench your own ride will be in this book.

After you've drained the oil in your bike and it's time to refill the oil, how many quarts will you fill it back up with? The answer is in the book. When you're checking the tension on your primary chain, how much free play should the primary chain have? It's in the book. How many pounds of air should be in the tires? You got it, it's in the book!

When I was in junior high doing homework at night I would occasionally ask my mom how to spell a word I was working on. The answer I would always get from Mom was, "Look it up in the dictionary." I hated that. But I'm glad she taught me the patience of having to look things up myself, because every day I am looking in the shop manuals for specs or other information needed to do the job right.

Let's get familiar with the service manual. Up front you'll find a table of contents broken down into sections. Each different section will be broken down into categories specific to the area the section is covering. Usually at the beginning of each section you'll find the specifications. These specs contain important information such as the correct amount of air to have in your tires and torque specs for the front

The service manual is the bible of wrenching. You'll be using this book for every task you perform on your bike. If you don't already have a service manual for your motorcycle and want to start wrenching on your bike, then now is the time to go get one.

The service interval chart is a great quick reference for service intervals at listed mileage. Use this for regular scheduled maintenance.

An owner's manual is very different from the service manual. Every new bike comes equipped with one. The owner's manual is loaded with useful information, and newer models have service intervals listed by mileage with a convenient checklist. This book is more of an operations manual than a repair manual.

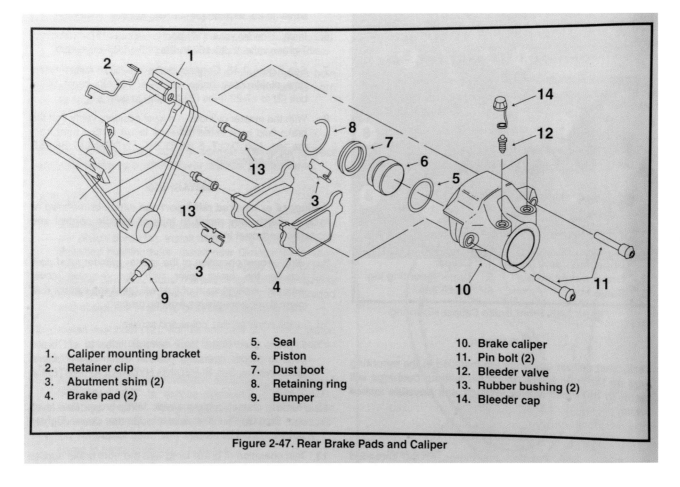

1. Caliper mounting bracket
2. Retainer clip
3. Abutment shim (2)
4. Brake pad (2)
5. Seal
6. Piston
7. Dust boot
8. Retaining ring
9. Bumper
10. Brake caliper
11. Pin bolt (2)
12. Bleeder valve
13. Rubber bushing (2)
14. Bleeder cap

Figure 2-47. Rear Brake Pads and Caliper

You'll find information like this throughout your owner's manual. Exploded views and all sorts of useful information are great to help you locate an item you might otherwise have trouble finding.

axle—important things. The back of the book will have an index. So if you're not sure where to find something you can look up the word directly and find a page number to take you right to it.

The manual isn't going to be a book that you sit down and read cover to cover. This is a reference book like a dictionary, something you use when you need to look up information. However, if you want to get a heads-up on your bike's operating systems then go ahead and give the service manual a read. Some of the information may be a bit too technical for a novice, but you have to remember that these books are for factory-trained mechanics who have taken classes in this field. So don't be surprised if you find scenarios such as spacing transmission gears and setting bearing clearance too intimidating. Just remember there are also many diagrams and operating principles for many systems, as well as troubleshooting charts, that could help you resolve a mechanical issue without taking it to the mechanic and spending a ton of money. Some

publishers, such as Clymer, publish repair manuals that are intended to be used by the novice wrencher, so things may be spelled out a little more clearly for you.

In the service manual you'll also find warnings and cautions. Please pay attention to these, they were included for a reason. A warning may indicate a potentially hazardous situation that could result in a serious injury or worse. These warnings may vary in severity. Sometimes it's meant to protect a part on the bike, and sometimes it's meant to protect you in the shop or on the road. There are many dangers to consider: A hot part, a tightly compressed spring, flammable liquids, a part that might come loose at high speeds, the list is endless. So pay attention because the writers of your manual included those warnings for a reason.

The first thing I do before performing a task on my bike is grab my shop manual. I hope you'll get into the same routine. If the service manual is right there next to you then you really have no excuse for not getting the proper information. Maintaining your bike should be fun, and part of the independent feeling we get when we ride comes from knowing we've been smart and safe in our maintenance.

HOW TO USE THE PARTS BOOK

A parts book is available for all models and is great to have on hand for exploded views of internal parts, the parts you can't see but know are there. The parts book will have all seals, O-rings, bearings, etc., listed in the exploded view with a letter or number referencing a chart of original equipment manufacturer (OEM) numbers. These OEM numbers are what you will use when re-ordering a part needed for repair.

Another great quality of the parts book is the description or name of parts. When you find what you're looking for in the parts book "that thing by the round part" will have a name for you to reference it with, such as a main shaft seal or trans-roller bearing. This comes in handy when ordering parts. A parts salesperson will have a much easier time trying to locate a starter shaft lock tab rather than a "metal piece with a notch on it."

Being prepared with the OEM part numbers and other information is part of having as much knowledge on hand as you can to get the job done right. You need to be parts savvy. It's a big piece of the puzzle when maintaining your own bike. If you don't use the right part, you may do some serious damage to your bike or hurt yourself when riding.

Above: Publishers such as Clymer and Haynes print repair manuals for many makes and models of motorcycles, providing an alternative to factory service manuals for late-model bikes as well as manuals for models no longer in production. Right: With any task you perform on your bike, your service manual should be the first tool you grab.

CHAPTER 2
TOOL TIME

BASIC SET OF TOOLS TO HAVE ON HAND

If you're going to take on the responsibility of maintaining your own bike, then we need to get you hooked up with a slick set of tools. There are two sets of tools: American, measured in inches, and metric, measured in millimeters. I primarily work with American motorcycles. Depending on your bike you may use a metric set of tools. Check your service manual and make sure you're using the right tools.

It's important to buy from a reputable manufacturer of quality tools. There are plenty to choose from. I recommend Sears Craftsman. Why? Because Sears has an actual storefront, versus companies like Snap-on, Matco, or MAC, which normally sell via catalog, websites, or a truck that stops by businesses. If you want one of these trucks to stop by your home, check out the company's website for more

information. Be forewarned, however. Walking inside those tool trucks is very dangerous. Even if you don't consider yourself to be a compulsive shopper, you will become one when you see all those shiny tools so neatly displayed.

I also recommend using a quality tool like Sears because of the lifetime guarantee they provide. The other tool suppliers I mentioned also have a lifetime guarantee, as will any reputable tool company. If you should break a tool or if the tool fails you in any way you can bring it right back in and get it replaced for free. What's nice about using a storefront brand is that you can run out and replace it quickly rather than waiting for a delivery truck.

We'll start with a ratchet and socket set, probably the most valuable thing in your tool collection. You'll use a ratchet and socket for almost every project.

Once you have your tools, keep them organized and neat for easy access and quick identification. Take pride in keeping your tools organized—it will pay off when you're searching for one in a hurry.

You'll need to determine whether open-end wrenches or box-end wrenches will best suit the job you are doing.

You want to make sure the drive of the ratchet mates up with the drive on the socket. If you're buying a complete set, it's all matched up for you. For most American-type bikes, a set ranging from ¼-inch to 1¼-inch will be great.

Not all bolts on the bike will be hex heads, so you'll want a few different wrenches. A very popular style of bolt head is the Allen head. You can buy sockets with Allens on the end to fit in your ratchet or simply buy an Allen key kit. Allen keys are L-shaped keys of different sizes, usually clipped together, with hex-shaped ends. A kit ranging from ⁵⁄₆₄-inch to ⅜-inch will be a good range for American-built bikes.

Another bolt head type is the torx, with little star-shaped holes that require a special set of sockets or keys, like Allen heads. Torx bolts are measured differently and come in sizes with a "T" in front of the number. Instead of being measured in inches or millimeters, they have a size value all their own. A set of wrenches or keys ranging from T10 to T50 is good to have on hand.

Torx bolts are the easiest to strip out, which is a great recipe for cursing and wrench throwing. If you find yourself stripping a bolt, whatever size or type, you're in for a boatload of fun! A good way to prevent a bolt from stripping out is to make sure the tool is in the head of the bolt all the way and to turn slowly. If you feel the tool start to skip or turn without moving the bolt, STOP. Don't go any farther until you get some help from someone with more experience in stubborn bolts.

Certain jobs you'll be performing on your bike will require you to torque the bolts. You can purchase a torque wrench at Sears or through any of the tool suppliers I mentioned above. Torque wrenches come in different drive sizes (e.g., ¼-inch, ⅜-inch, or ½-inch) and within the different sizes they have different torque ranges. The best thing to do before you purchase a torque wrench is to check your service manual for the torque range required for the job you'll be doing. Usually the larger wrenches are for the wheels and smaller ones are for engines and other tight places. A torque wrench works by setting the desired torque value on the wrench, and as you tighten the wrench up to that value it will make a clicking sound to indicate it's tightened.

While most motorcycle projects will involve bolts of different sizes and types, it goes without saying that any good toolkit should include some good old-fashioned screwdrivers, Phillips and standard, of varying sizes. A set of jeweler's screwdrivers, the real tiny ones, is also a good thing to have.

Line wrenches are normally used for working on fittings or brake lines. Line wrenches allow maximum contact while fitting over the brake or fuel line.

Ratchet wrenches are great for a long bolt that you'll be turning for a while. They're not a necessity, but they do help to speed up a job.

There are two types of torque wrenches, the beam-type (left) and the click-type (middle and right).

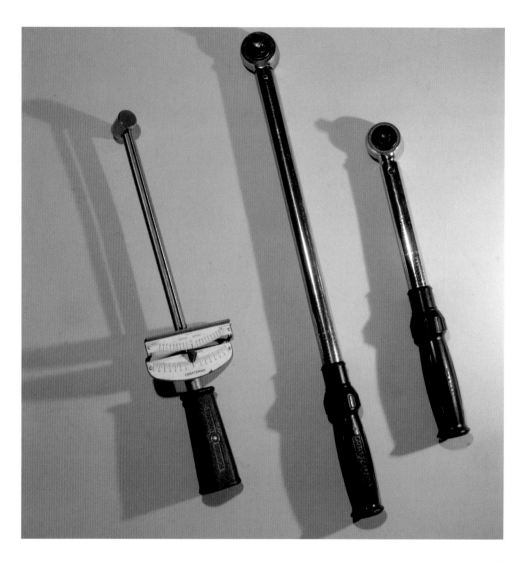

The lower scale on the beam-type torque wrench is in foot-pounds and the upper is in metric Newton-meters. Both specs are generally printed in the service manual. As you tighten the bolt, you simply watch the scale until you reach the required spec.

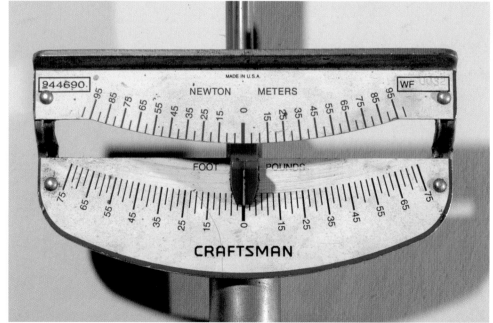

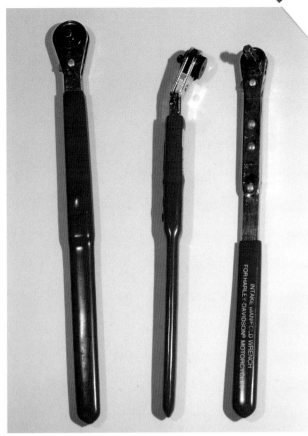

Above left: The same measurement scales are shown on the click-type torque wrench. These wrenches are set to the specified torque prior to use. Once proper torque is achieved you will feel and hear a "click." Above right: Tool manufactures such as JIMS and Kastar have developed specialty tools to fit specific areas of American V-Twin engines. Shown here are a ratcheting rocker box wrench, a ³⁄₁₆-inch ball-end Allen wrench, and a ¼-inch ball-end intake wrench. (The ³⁄₁₆-inch ball-end Allen wrench is sold as a speedometer sensor wrench but is useful in many hard to reach applications.)

You'll also want a set of pliers, standard and needle-nose, to hold onto anything that wants to get away from you. A set of locking pliers or Vise-Grips is good for working on something that you'll need two free hands for. Your pliers will help to grab things in places your fingers won't fit. A set of wire cutters or diagonals are great if you need to cut a wire or a zip tie that you've used to temporarily hold something.

You should also have a set of open- and closed-end wrenches on hand. Battery terminals on American bikes use a metric size, so make sure you get a 10-mm open-end wrench for that job.

You will also need an oil filter wrench, several types of which are available. Pick one that suits your bike best. Band type, strap type, or end-cap type. Some motorcycle manufacturers offer an oil filter wrench specifically made for your bike and filter. Make sure you also have a tire pressure gauge and oil drain pain.

A voltage meter is one tool that will make troubleshooting so much easier. It's what you will use if you need to check the voltage of your battery or want to inspect your charging system. A test light is also good to have on hand to test for wire continuity.

MOTORCYCLE SPECIALTY TOOLS

In your shop manual you will find a tools section and a list of all specialty tools (with part numbers) required for certain tasks. You won't need these tools for basic service but if you find yourself feeling confident, and able to use your service manual, this is where you can find the right tool for the job. JIMS is a manufacturer of motorcycle specialty tools, and you can order these at any Harley-Davidson dealer or aftermarket shop.

I don't recommend just going out and buying these tools to have on hand. They can get expensive, and they're usually only used for a specific job. If you find yourself with a repair job, take the time to look in your service manual for the tools needed for the task. If a specialty tool is listed, then it's a good time to invest in the tool. Make sure you read

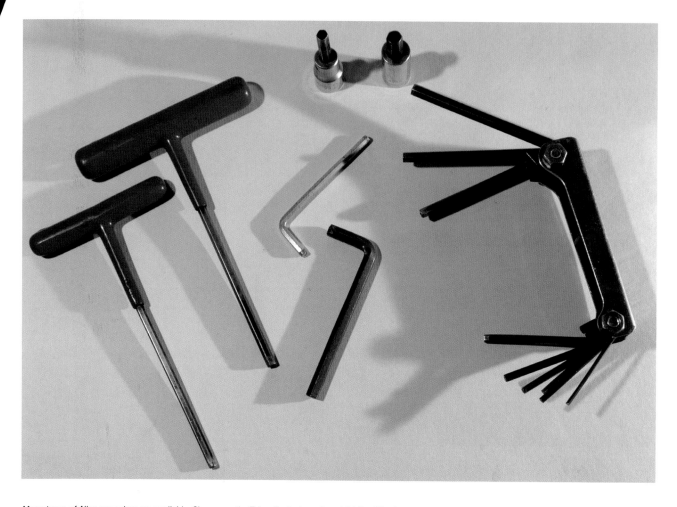

Many types of Allen wrenches are available. Shown are the T-handle, L-shaped, and folding Allen key kit. It's nice to have the different styles on hand for unique situations.

Just as the Allen wrenches exist in many different forms, so do Torx-style wrenches: socket-types for ratchet drives, folding kits, a screwdriver-type handle, as well as L-type and T-handles.

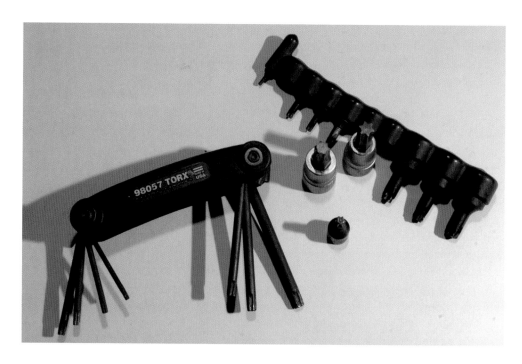

Impact drivers are used for stubborn or stuck bolts, providing a shock of quick twisting motion to the bolt. First, the appropriate socket is attached to the end of the driver. The tool is inserted into or around the bolt. Next, the body of the driver is twisted in the desired direction of removal. A hammer is used to strike the butt-end of the driver, multiplying the torque to turn the bolt loose.

about the job you're going to do in your service manual for any of these motorcycle-specific tools before you start the job. You never want to find yourself halfway into a job only to realize you don't have a clutch hub puller or a bearing install tool needed to finish the job.

BIKE LIFTS AND THE WORK AREA

Now that you plan to work on your own bike and have some tools ready to do the job, it's time to set up your work area. Most people will use their garage or tool shed for their workspace. This is probably your best bet. I recommend that you don't work in a space close to a water heater or furnace, such as your basement. If you ask around, you're bound to hear at least one story of a water heater kicking on just as fuel was spilled or a gas can was opened and the obvious tragedy followed. Trust me, it happens.

When you get your location picked out, make sure the area is well lit. There is nothing worse than spending hours trying to find that locknut you dropped. Design your workspace with plenty of lighting and electrical outlets, and eliminate the clumsiness of tripping over extension cords. If you have to heat the space, use a heat source that will be safe with no open flame. A wood burner is not the best heat source for a motorcycle shop.

Notice the difference between the Torx (star-shaped) and the Allen. Sometimes at quick glance you could mistake which tool is needed and risk stripping out the head of the bolt.

If you are building a workspace from the ground up, make sure you plan ahead and think about the location. Don't build out in the middle of your backyard forcing you to ride across a jungle to get to it. If you're building from the ground up, be sure to build on a solid concrete foundation. If you're going through all the trouble of building up a space, you might as well build one that will last.

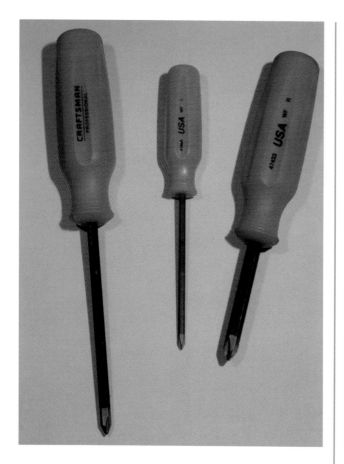

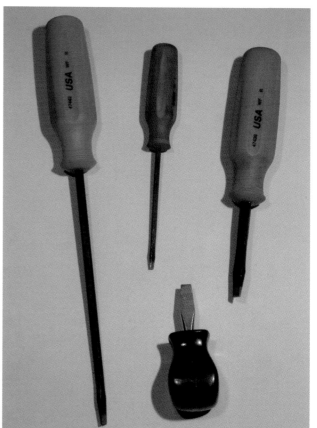

Flathead screwdrivers (above) need no explanation, but they're a necessity in your tool box. Above right: You should never interchange screwdriver types. Don't use a flathead screwdriver on a Phillips-style screw, or vice versa.

Keep your area clean. By keeping your work area clean you are eliminating the most common problems, such as dirt and debris, from finding their way into your engine or primary when you have it apart. Get yourself proper containers with spill-proof caps for storing used fluids and transporting them to the recycling center. Keep on top of the cleaning of your shop. It doesn't take very long for trash and dirt to accumulate and cause clutter, leading to a very non-welcoming work environment.

If you can set your shop up with good shelving or a pegboard wall go ahead and do it. Being organized is a big challenge in a motorcycle workspace and you'll need a safe place to store parts and tools.

Last but not least, safety must take top priority in your workshop. You don't want gasoline near open flames or anything creating a spark. A metal trashcan is good to have for disposal of oily rags or old aerosol cans. The two most important items you must have on hand in your workspace are a fire extinguisher and a first-aid kit. Accidents do and will happen and it's so important to be prepared as well as you can.

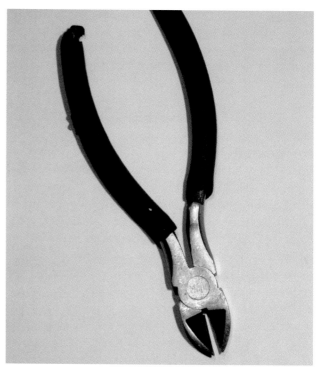

Here is a set of diagonals referred to as "dykes." Notice the slant, or diagonal, perfect for cutting wire zip ties.

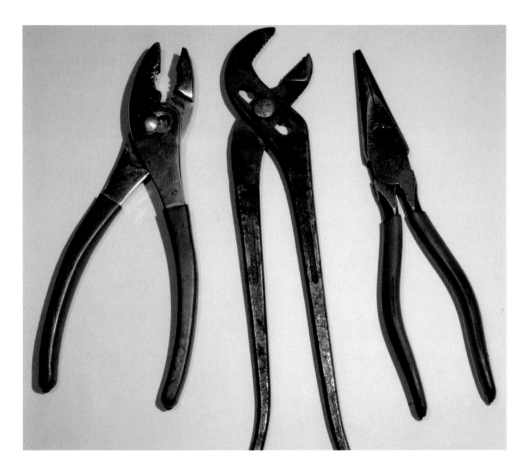

You'll want to have a few different types of pliers in your tool box: standard, channel lock, and needle nose provide easy access in different situations.

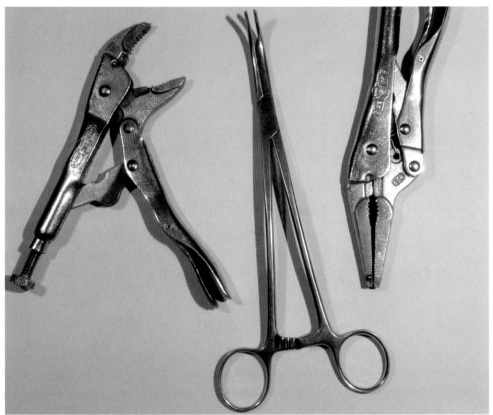

Vise grips are great for holding something in place that you can't afford to drop or keep chasing when it slips away.

31

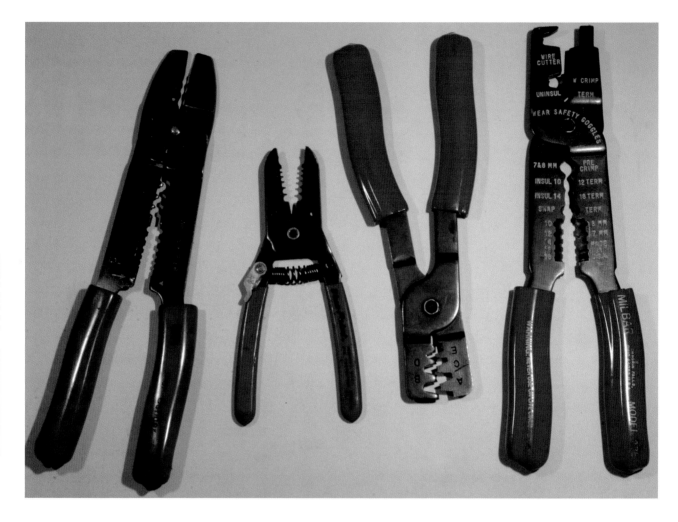

Wire strippers and crimping tools are needed for any electrical work on your bike. Certain wire terminals need a specific tool for proper crimping.

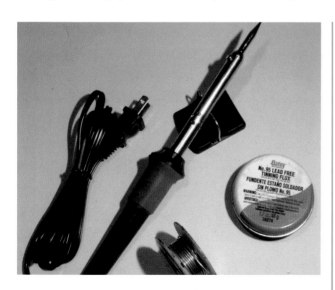

The needle and thread of wire repair. If you will be doing any wiring on your bike, you will want to have a soldering gun, solder, and flux on hand. Don't forget the shrink tubing for wire insulation.

If you have some extra cash, a bike lift is a great investment. A bike lift makes service work much easier and you won't end up like a contortionist trying to reach oddly positioned bolts on your bike. The lift will put the bike up in the air and make it much more accessible. Another great feature of the lift is the ease of cleaning your bike, especially your wheels.

Many different types of lifts are available and you don't necessarily have to buy the most expensive lift, but the least expensive lift may not be the best deal either. Certain model bikes, such as certain Dynas and Sportsters, have uneven undersides and need frame adapters to lift the bike level. Not all lifts have these available. Make sure you tell the salesperson selling you the lift what type of bike you have. You also want to make sure the lift you're buying is rated for the correct weight of your bike; you can find the weight of your bike in your service manual.

Don't skimp out on a lift, quality rules over price like anything in life. You don't want to be trusting a $99 lift to

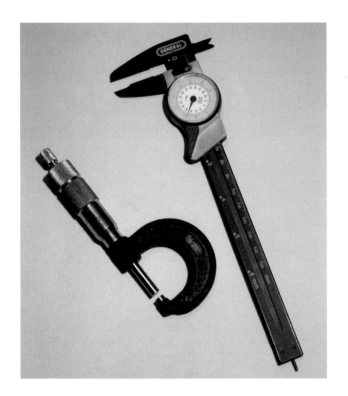

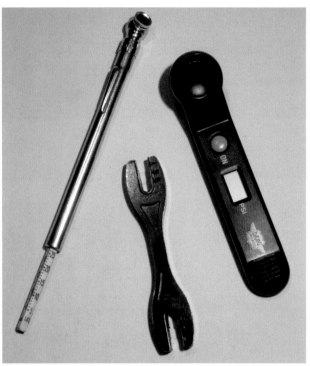

Above left: These tools are mostly used in measuring clearances and shims. They also work well for checking brake pad thickness, if you want to get technical.
Above right: A tire gauge is essential. You'll use this tool daily to check the air pressure in your tires. Buy a spoke wrench if you have spoked wheels. Checking spokes for tightness is also an important part of servicing your bike.

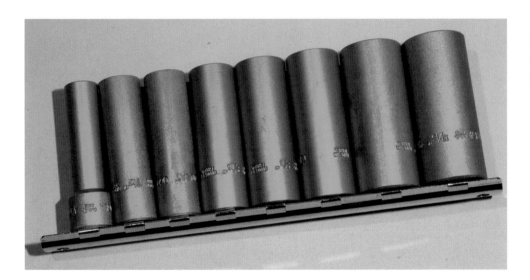

The blue anodized-aluminum sockets shown here are for low torque applications on chrome-plated fasteners.

support your bike only because it was a great bargain. Remember, this lift is going to be holding anywhere from 500 to 800 pounds of bike 12 to 24 inches in the air, and you will be right next to or underneath it. If that lift fails where's your value now? You'll be spending more money on repairs to the bike from the damage it sustained in the fall, and that's hoping you got away clean without any damage yourself. When shopping for a lift, you want to buy one that will lift your bike, balance it properly and safely, and will serve you for many years to come.

Any bike shop, dealer, or aftermarket will have lifts for sale or at least have a catalog to order one for you. Handy Industries sells great floor-jack-style motorcycle lifts and, if you have the room, table lifts.

Make sure you have some good-quality tie-downs in the garage to hold the bike safely when on the lift. Tie-downs

Oil filter wrenches are available in strap or band styles. You'll need to determine which suits you and your model best. Oil filter ramps make the filter change less messy by catching the old oil and directing it to the drain pan as the filter is removed.

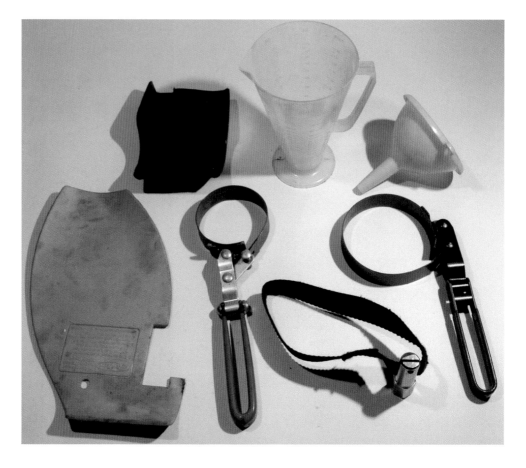

This smaller socket and ratchet set is a great tool kit to have in your garage. The smaller ratchet helps in those hard to reach areas found all over the motorcycle.

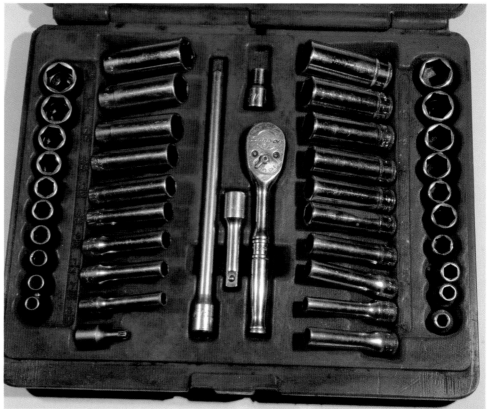

Here are your typical ratchet and sockets. You can purchase a starter set and add on as you need additional sockets and extensions.

It's a good idea to have a set of tie-downs on hand. If you have a bike lift, always secure the bike to the lift with tie-downs. If you need to put your bike in a truck or trailer, you'll also need tie-downs. Soft straps help protect chrome and painted surfaces.

A battery tender is one of the most important tools in your garage. You'll use this to maintain the voltage of your battery during storage or extended parking

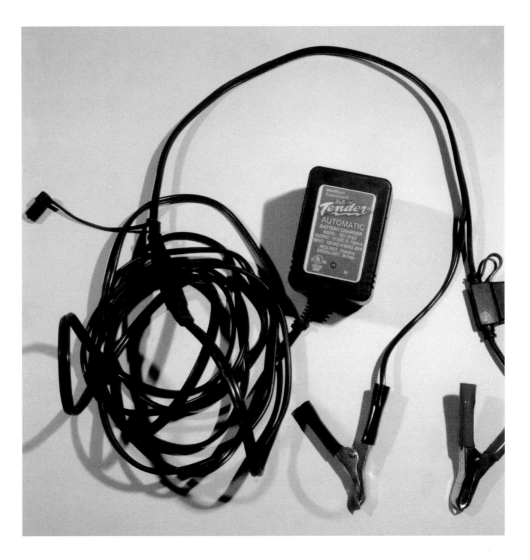

A volt meter (left) comes in handy for testing voltage and troubleshooting electrical components. A test light (right) is used to test for power and continuity.

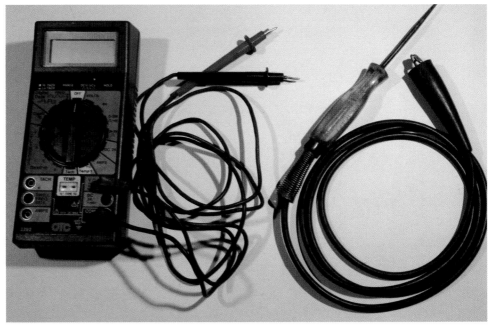

A spark plug gap tool is an essential tool. Keep one in your bike's tool kit for roadside plug changes.

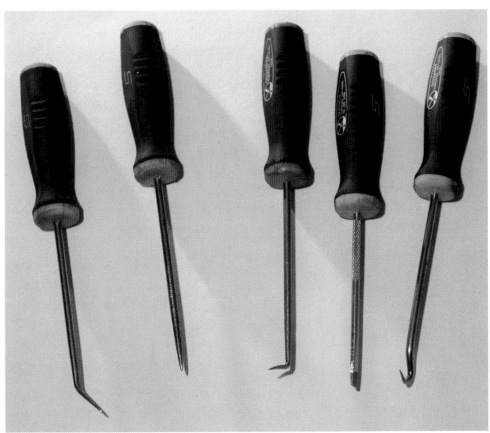

A unique tool kit, like this one packed with funky-shaped pick tools, will come in handy for removing odd circlips, O-rings, retaining clips, and more.

You should have various lubricants and sealants on hand in the garage. If bearings need repacking, you'll use a waterproof grease. Grip glue is great for installing new handgrips. Anti-seize is used to prevent bolts or axles from corrosion and becoming galled or seized. Hylomar sealer is great when replacing gaskets.

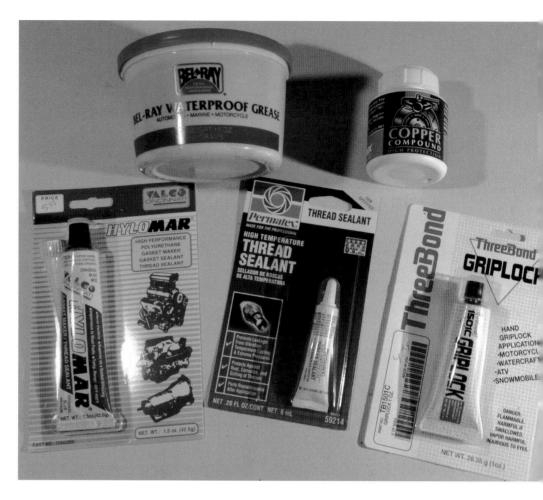

are also needed if you should ever trailer your bike to a shop, travel destination, or if you're picked up from a breakdown on the side of the road.

Go ahead and get yourself a toolbox or something to keep your tools organized in. Be creative; no one says you have to use the standard red box that most mechanics use.

Once you set up your work area with a lift and toolbox, make sure to allow yourself plenty of shelf space and clean areas to store parts you remove from your bike during your repair work. You don't want to be placing your fuel tank in the middle of the floor risking dents and scratches. Keep some Tupperware containers or plastic bags nearby for bolt storage. If you keep all the bolts you removed organized and labeled clearly, you won't be wasting hours trying to find one missing bolt to complete the job.

SOME MISCELLANEOUS TOOLS AND SUPPLIES YOU SHOULD HAVE ON HAND IN YOUR GARAGE

Safety glasses. Safety first!

Single-edge razor blades for various uses. You won't believe how indispensable razor blades are in the shop.

Bolt cutters. You'd be surprised . . .

A table vise. Holds parts in place while you work on them.

Various lengths of 2 x 4 or wooden blocks. Great for propping up a bike or as a buffer when hammering.

Plastic bags or Tupperware containers. Use these for separating and holding bolts.

Work gloves

Metal files

Dremel tool or die grinder

Hacksaw

Rivet gun and rivets

Air compressor and impact gun

Mallet

Mechanic's hammer

Carb and brake cleaner

General cleaning products

Wire brush

Sandpaper

Scotch Brite pads

Parts washer or small tub specifically for solvent use

Heat gun or small torch for shrink wrapping or heating any surface you need heated

Thread-lock is needed for replacing bolts on your bike. Your service manual will indicate which degree of hold to use. Red is high, blue is medium, and purple is light.

Below: You'd be surprised how easily a little bolt can get lost on your motorcycle. A flashlight is a great tool to shine some light in those hidden spots on your bike or the dark corners of your garage.

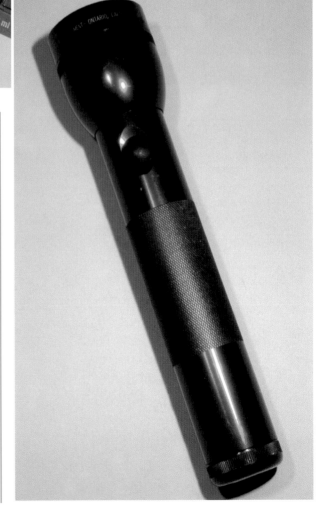

USING THE RIGHT TOOL FOR THE JOB

Now that you have the tools, let's talk about what they do and learn to avoid using them for the wrong job. When I first got into cars, tools, and hanging out in the garage with my dad, he would always tell me to use the right tool for the job. It sounds like common sense, but I will admit I have found myself being lazy and just grabbing any nearby tool to try to get the job done. Using the right tool for the job makes it go more smoothly and is the recipe for less frustration and wrench throwing. It will also help maintain the life and quality of the tool.

You may of heard of something called "wrench throwing." Wrench throwing happens because mechanical work is very frustrating and usually not a smooth operation. A job that seems so easy, maybe a half-hour's worth of work, could end up taking hours over one stupid little bolt that will mess up your whole day.

Here's a scenario: You find yourself cursing at some little bolt that's keeping you from moving forward with the job. Maybe you'll hit it with whatever tool you have in your hand. It still won't help. That bolt will continue to fight with you until you now find yourself sweating and cursing words you didn't even know existed, and then, to top it all

If it isn't hydraulic, a bike lift may require some manual effort on your part.

When doing a project that could take some time, a floor dolly such as this one works great and keeps your lift free for other uses.

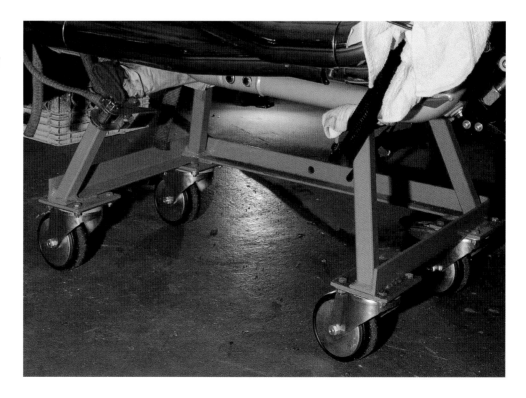

A jack lift makes lifting the bike a breeze by foot pumping the bottle jack. You can see this one has many years on it. Don't skimp when buying a lift, get one that will last.

off, the only way you know how to handle all the anger and frustration is to wail your tool across the floor.

There, that's better. Now you're ready to pick the tool up and start all over.

I hope you can keep away from situations like this while maintaining your own bike. But I'm not going to sugar coat this: Wrenching is not easy, and you will find yourself facing stubborn bolts or nuts here and there. I'm sorry to tell you there is no "magic" to make it better. Throughout the day I will usually get at least one phone call from a very irritated "self-wrencher" who has found himself at wit's end with a bolt or nut and is calling me to find out what to do to make the bolt or nut come loose. I feel bad, but most of the time I want to laugh. What do they think I'm going to tell them? "Say these magic words five times, turn around twice, and Bingo—that bolt will come out"? It's a bitch to wrench on something that won't cooperate, but it's part of wrenching.

You know the saying "take the good with the bad"? Eventually, after you take the time to slowly resolve the situation, when you finish and get the job done right, you'll be on cloud nine. The satisfaction of defeat over the stubborn bolt or nut is victorious. You'll feel like you just won the Daytona 500.

Before throwing in the towel, try simple solutions like using a longer wrench for better leverage or spraying a little WD40 or penetrating oil on the nut to see if it loosens. Never whack on a wrench with a hammer or mallet. This can strip the head off the bolt or ruin your tool.

Here are some of the important supplies you'll want in your work space. Always put them back where they came from for easy and quick grabbing.

If you have the room in your workspace, the best lift to have is a table lift. The bike will be at just the right height to work on. It's also convenient to have a surface to set your tools on.

Of course, if you find yourself in a no-win situation with something you're working on, the right thing to do is to make an appointment with your service shop. If you don't have the experience in dealing with stubborn situations like these be smart and get some help. It will keep your bike safe, probably keep you safe and not to mention it will save the poor wrench you're ready to wail across the floor, and anything that may get in its way.

CARE OF TOOLS

The next topic I want to talk about is really important, and I can't stress this enough: You must always inspect your tools for damage. If the tool is damaged, you don't want to use it. If you purchased your tools from a lifetime replacement company, take the tool back and get it replaced.

Sometimes a bad tool can be the culprit in ruining a job or a part. And you don't want to deal with that, do you? You don't want a bad tool causing you all that wasted time, stress, and cursing? You'll feel pretty lousy if a simple tool inspection could have prevented a day of hell in your garage.

Now that you have a nice set of tools, it's important to take care of them. Store them properly, clean them after use, and inspect them regularly. These are your tools. You are depending on these tools to help achieve the proper level of maintenance on your bike. These tools are ensuring you a safe ride, so respect them and take care of them.

When using wrenches, make sure the ratchet mechanisms are working properly. Never hammer on a wrench or strike it with any other tool. When working with screwdrivers, you never want to interchange the tip to the fastener. Never use a standard head on a Phillips fastener. Don't try to pry things with a screwdriver. If the screwdriver shows rounded edges, go ahead and replace it.

A mint-condition tool is key to getting the job done right with no cursing and no wrench throwing. This is where you'll be glad you took the time to get hooked up with a reputable tool company. If something happens to the tool it will be taken care of by the company you bought it from. Tools are a great investment, they are fun to have, and you'll be surprised how often you'll be using them. You will, without a doubt, get your money's worth in the first job you do on your bike alone.

This takes us back to the basics: Slow down, take your time, and inspect things thoroughly. You will apply this approach to everything related to maintaining your motorcycle, whether you're inspecting your riding gear, your tools, or your bike. You have to know what you're dealing with.

CHAPTER 3
DROP THAT FLUID

V-TWIN 4-STROKE UNDERSTANDING

Let's start by understanding the workings of the V-Twin engine. The V-Twin engine is a 4-stroke overhead valve engine. That means we have intake, compression, power, and exhaust. Those are your four "strokes."

When you fire your bike, the battery (the power source) powers the trigger mechanism or control unit that ignites the coil. The coil turns 12 volts of power into tens of thousands of volts, 50,000 or more, into the spark plug, which is under pressure.

Here's where the four strokes come in. On the intake stroke, as the piston moves downward it pulls the air-fuel mixture into the cylinder. At the bottom of the stroke as the piston then starts to travel back up, the intake valve is closing at this time and the air-fuel mixture is compressed in the combustion chamber. This is the compression stroke. Next, just as the piston is reaching top dead center (TDC) of the compression stroke, the spark plug fires, igniting the air-fuel mixture, which causes an explosion and pushes the piston downward, making this the power stroke. On returning up in the cylinder from the power stroke, the burned air-fuel mixture is expelled through the now-open exhaust valve. This is obviously the exhaust stroke.

When the piston moves, it pushes the connecting rods that turn the engine crank (bottom end). The cam gear is driven off of the crankshaft pinion gear. The camshaft has an eccentric lobe (shaped like an egg) that rotates and pushes upward on the valve lifter. The pushrod connects the lifter to the rocker arm, a lever that changes the upward movement of the pushrod to downward pressure to open the valve and repeat the four-stroke process all over again.

All of this work has to happen at the right time. This is all happening rather fast, about 1,000 rotations a minute at idle speed. If the engine has had a performance cam installed, it will require a faster idle speed than stock. For every rotation of the flywheel, the piston moves up and down once, which means the piston moves twice as many times as the crankshaft at any given rpm.

With your engine working that hard, you can see why proper maintenance is very important. You want that engine in top running condition. Imagine trying to run a marathon and not training at all for the run. No exercise, no practice running, no stretching, no cardio training, nothing. Top that all off with not eating for a few days prior to the event. The body is going to fail and you will not finish running that marathon. If you don't keep your engine maintained or "trained" it's going to fail just like your body would.

So, now that we know why we need to maintain our bikes, let's start with the basics of how we do it.

THE OIL SYSTEM

The V-Twin engine in your bike uses a force-feed or pressure-type oil pump setup. Your oil pump works by gravity moving the oil from the oil tank to the pump inlet. The oil pump creates pressure, forcing oil into the engine. This lubricates the lower end, connecting rod, bearings, rocker arm bushings, valve stems, pushrods, and tappets. The cylinder walls, pistons, and timing gears are lubed by oil spray thrown off connecting rods and the crankshaft. They are also lubed by oil draining from the rocker boxes through an internal drain passage in each cylinder and tappet guide. The "scavenging" portion of the pump removes excess oil from the engine, passes it through the filter, and returns it to the tank to start the process over again.

Make sure you have everything on hand for the job you're about to perform.

PROJECT 1 | Oil and Filter Change

Tools Needed: Filter wrench, wrench or socket sized for your drain plug, small socket or screwdriver (on models equipped with a drain hose), drain pan, brake cleaner, shop towels

Time: About 20 minutes, start to finish   **Talent:** Beginner

Cost: Depends on the oil you choose: Synthetic oil and filter: $60.00, Standard oil and filter: $30.00

Parts required: 3–4 quarts oil (depending on the model), drain pan, oil filter

Performance Gain: Clean oil is good for an engine. You won't be gaining any horsepower, but you'll help prolong the life of your engine.

change my oil every 2,500 miles, sometimes sooner. I guess it depends on the riding I'm doing. Since I've been running the shop, I don't get to ride as much as I want so it's been more of a scheduled routine for me.

If you don't put on a lot of miles, change the oil at least twice a year. If you're doing some heavy riding, especially in warm climates, you might want to change the oil sooner. It's not expensive to change the oil, especially if you're doing it yourself. It's the best thing you can do to help prolong the life of your engine; it always helps and never hurts, so do it as often as you like.

The first thing to do is get your service manual and locate your drain plug for the engine oil. The drain plug is going to be located in different areas from model to model. On Softails, the drain plug is usually at the end of the drain hose attached to the frame or is plugged to the frame. On Sportster models, the drain hose is plugged to the frame or the battery box. On very early Sportster models, the drain

On this Sportster, the oil drain hose is plugged off to the frame. Each model's drain is located differently, and your service manual will point out its location.

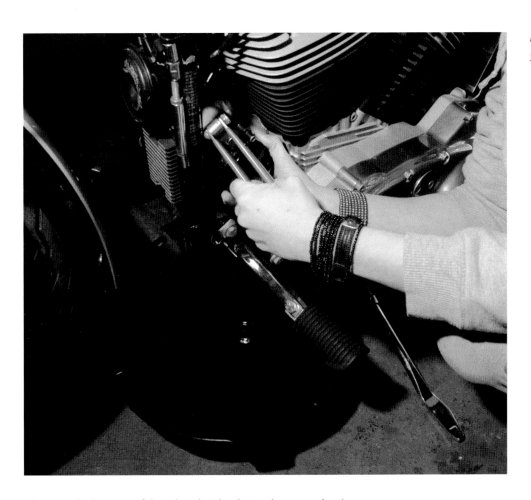

Pick an oil filter wrench that fits your bike best.

plug is at the bottom of the oil tank. The drain plug on early FL models is located at the bottom of the oil tank as well.

On later FL models, the oil tank was moved and is mounted under the transmission. Dyna models use the same setup. Be sure to check your service manual and locate the correct drain plug, as the oil and transmission drain plugs are located next to each other on these two models.

If your engine is cool, you'll want to fire it up to warm the oil and get the flow moving more smoothly before draining it. Shut off the engine, set your drain pan underneath the bike at the draining area, and let the oil drain into the pan. Once the oil starts to pour into the drain pan, go ahead and lift the oil-tank cap to help get the oil flowing faster.

You'll find in the service manual that your next step is to take the oil filter off and clean the area of old oil residue. On earlier models, the oil filter will be a drop-in style that goes directly into the oil tank. If you have a second drain pan, place that underneath your oil filter. If you only have one pan, wait until the oil is done draining from the bike, replace your drain plug, then move your drain pan under the oil filter. I recommend you replace the drain plug before moving the drain pan so you don't accidentally refill the oil while the drain plug is still out.

Don't forget to have the drain pan underneath to catch the excess oil while removing the filter.

Refer to your manual for correct oil fill amounts. Too much oil is just as bad as too little.

Newer motorcycles will have an external twist-on-style oil filter. If that's what you have, get your oil filter wrench and place it around the filter and break the filter loose. Once the oil filter is removed, oil is going to pour down the bike. You can buy plastic oil filter draining sleeves or "ramps," but a piece of cardboard bent just the right way works just as well. Brake cleaner or carb cleaner works well for oil cleanup. Use one of these to clean old oil from the oil filter housing and wipe the area clean.

When the bike is done draining, clean the threads on the plug before replacing it, and replace any O-rings if your bike uses them. When replacing the new oil filter, take some fresh oil on your finger and lube the top of your oil filter. This helps create a seal and makes it easier to remove the filter down the road. Using a few drops of fresh oil, go ahead and pour a few drops inside the new filter, then screw the filter back onto the filter housing.

Do not tighten the filter with the wrench, only hand tighten it ¾ to 1 full turn once it's secure. Refer to your service manual for your fluid fill amount specs and go ahead and refill the oil using a funnel in the oil tank.

Synthetic vs. Standard Oil

A topic that seems to be on everyone's mind these days is what type of oil to use. I have discussions like this with customers probably a dozen times a day: synthetic or standard, or blend. What's the difference? Which is better?

Synthetic oils are better in almost every aspect, which is why they cost more. Synthetics typically have lower volatility, meaning they offer more resistance to burn off and lower pour points, meaning better low-temperature lubrication characteristics. Additionally, synthetic oils are more resilient to oxidation, so they will last longer than a petroleum-based product. Synthetic oils also have a tendency to keep engines clean from deposit buildup.

Some people would like to have some of the advantages of synthetic oil without the price tag. This is why some oil companies offer semi-synthetic (aka synthetic blend) oils. Semi-synthetic oil is simply a compromise between fully synthetic oil and petroleum oil.

You can see there's a big difference between synthetic oil and standard oil. Advantages and disadvantages to both. But let's get some basics down to help you decide. Hey, it's your bike, and you're going to need to decide what to feed it, like you do your own body. Do you want to eat fast-food junk or something a little healthier?

First, whether you use synthetic or standard oil, it must be motorcycle-specific oil, not automotive. The chemistry make-up is different, and motorcycle oil has a zinc additive whereas automotive oil does not due to the catalytic converters in automobiles. Automobile oils are designed to meet fuel economy standards and they are limited as to what type of additives they can contain. A small amount of oil consumption is typical in autos, and oils with certain additives will poison a catalytic converter. Motorcycle oils are not faced with these limitations, so they are designed solely around performance. Most importantly, motorcycles utilize wet-clutch systems, whereas autos do not. A wet-clutch is a clutch that is bathed and cooled in the motor or transmission oil. Motorcycle oil has to be able to provide superior lubrication to transmission and engine components while also offering traction to the wet clutch to prevent slippage. This is a unique challenge that automobile oils aren't designed to handle. This is why motorcycle oil is more expensive than automotive oil.

The chemistry makeup is the big difference between synthetic and standard motorcycle oil as well. Both are fine to use, and this will be something you'll want to research for yourself.

One thing I do want to stress is that some oil manufacturers are recommending you can use synthetic oil in both the engine and transmission. I do not recommend this and will always advise people to use transmission oil in the transmission. Motorcycle oil companies such as Bel-Ray formulate oils specifically for use in the transmission. These oils are treated with additives that are designed to handle the shearing forces of gears and the extreme pressures found on the gear teeth. A bit of performance can be gained by using these oils, and the transmission fluids definitely prolong the life of the motorcycle by reducing transmission wear. I use Bel-Ray fluids in my bike, have been for years, and that's what I like.

You need to decide what type of oil you want to use and stick with that. It's your bike, so do your homework and decide which lubricant will be best for you.

A last word of caution: It's important to refill your oil according to the specs in your service manual. Too much oil is just as bad as too little oil. Like any other liquid, when the oil is under pressure it will find the quickest way out of the engine, which usually means a blown gasket or worse.

PROJECT 2	TP Smart Oil Pump Upgrade

Tools Needed: Drill, Allen wrenches, snap-ring pliers, ⁷⁄₁₆-inch wrench, screwdriver, drain pan, and shop rags

Time: Roughly 2–4 hours, start to finish   **Talent:** Intermediate

Cost: TP Smart Pump retails at $459 with breather, $359 without

Parts required: Permatex High-Temp thread sealant (part number 59235, do not use plumbing tape), SAE J1019 ⅜-inch 400-psi hose drain pan, shop rags

Performance Gain: Oil will now be delivered to the bottom end of your engine at idle speed and run through the filter before it enters the engine. This will help prolong the life of your engine.

One easy way to keep your bike's oiling system working in top condition is to upgrade the oil pump. The stock oil pump on Evo and Shovelhead engines does not deliver oil to the lower end at idle speeds. That means while you're sitting in traffic your engine is not getting oil delivered to the bottom end.

The smart oil pump from TP (Total Performance) is a great oil-system upgrade project for Evo and Shovelhead engines. The original TP Pro Series three-valve oil pump was designed to supply a constant flow of oil to both the top end and the bottom end at all engine-operating speeds. Stock oil pumps on Evo and Shovelheads shut off the flow of oil to the bottom end until approximately 1,800 rpm in order to direct 100 percent of the pump's output to the top end. The original Pro-Series oil pump by TP directs a portion of its output to the bottom end at low rpms in order to keep crankshaft and connecting-rod bearings lubricated, and thereby cooler.

The Twin-Cam engines were introduced in 1999 with a new lubricating system. The new system uses an internal oil pump and, unlike previous versions, it uses the feed side of the pump to force oil through the oil filter on its way into the engine. Since this approach removes any restriction on the oil-return line back to the oil-storage tank, the problem of oil remaining in the crankcase is eliminated, and a finer filter element may be used.

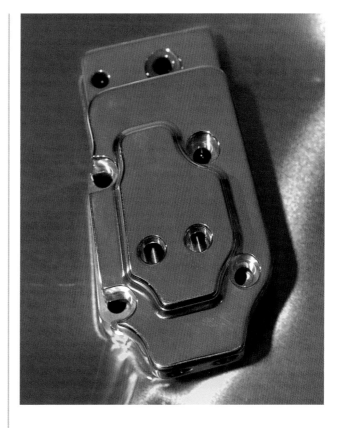

The TP smart oil pump is the best way to improve your oiling system.

More than likely you'll start this TP smart pump upgrade by removing the exhaust for access.

Harley-Davidson created a 10-micron oil filter for Twin-Cam engines to replace the previous 40-micron version used on Evolutions and earlier engine designs. While this filter traps smaller particles than were previously possible, it is not substantially different from the 40-micron version. When used on engines oher than Twin-Cams, it restricts oil return sufficiently enough to cause the crankcase to fill with oil and be forced through any available exit from the engine.

By installing the TP Pro-Series smart pump on this 1976 Shovelhead, it will provide a new passage to route oil from the pump's feed side to the oil filter and back before lubricating the engine, similar to the way a Twin-Cam pump operates. We can now use the finer 10-micron oil filters without the worry of the crankcase filling with oil.

Step-by-Step

Before we begin the upgrade, you'll have to drain the oil from the bike and have your service manual close by.

Next, remove the oil lines from the oil pump and the plug, and drain the oil from the feed line. Remove the oil-pump cover bolts, cover, and gasket. Next, remove the lock clip from the end of the oil-pump driveshaft, pull both gears from the pump body, and remove the oil-pump

Have your drain pan under the pump before disconnecting the oil lines and plug and draining oil from the feed line.

Carefully remove the pump cover bolts, cover, and old gasket.

driveshaft key from the driveshaft. Remove the two top bolts from the oil-pump body and slide it off the oil-pump driveshaft, then slide the remaining return gear off the oil-pump driveshaft and remove the driveshaft key.

We are not replacing the driveshaft, so that will stay in place. If your driveshaft was damaged and needs replacing, you will find instructions on how to replace it supplied with the kit.

Next, install the snap ring on the end of the oil-pump driveshaft. Install the new key in driveshaft for the return drive gear. The key will fit in the slot nearest the engine case. Slide the 0.625-inch oil return drive gear (larger of the set) on the driveshaft and over the key. Make sure the key stays in place and locks the gear to the shaft. Lubricate the idler shafts in both sides of the oil-pump body with assembly lube.

The next step is to install the new 0.625-inch return idler gear onto the idle shaft in the pump housing. Use a drop of blue Locktite on the bolts supplied for assembly. Use the new gasket supplied with the kit, making sure all holes line up with the pump. Use two hex-head top bolts to hold the gasket in place on the oil-pump body. You can use a dab of Hylomar gasket sealer to help keep that gasket from moving on you.

This step is a little tricky, so have your eye protection on when removing the lock clip from the end of the oil pump driveshaft.

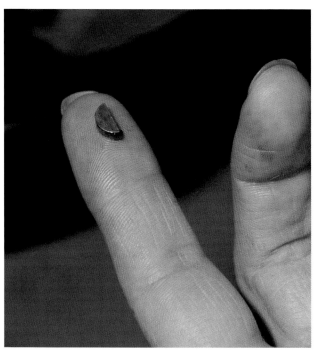

Carefully pull both gears from the pump body, and the driveshaft key from the driveshaft.

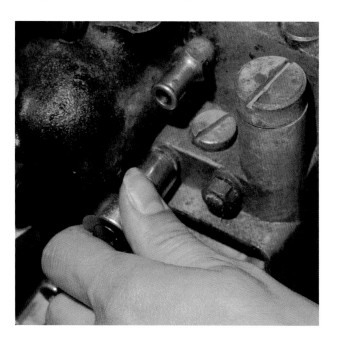

Carefully remove the stock oil pump body from the driveshaft once the two top bolts have been removed.

Slide the pump down the driveshaft while meshing the two return gears together. Lightly snug the two top bolts to hold the pump in place. Install the new key in the driveshaft for the feed gear. While holding the end of the driveshaft on the inside of the cam chest, slide the 0.500-inch feed drive gear (thinner of the gears) on the driveshaft, aligning the key with the cutout in the gear.

Go ahead and install the 0.500-inch pump feed idler gear onto the idle shaft in the pump body. Place the retaining clip on the end of driveshaft. Be sure to clean the gasket

Remove the old gasket, and use a single-edge razor or gasket scraper to remove any old gasket remaining.

Next slide the ⅝-inch oil return drive gear (the larger of the set) on the driveshaft over the key. This can be a little tricky, so make sure the key stays in place and locks the gear to the shaft.

Above: Notice the difference between the gears supplied in the TP smart oil pump. Right: Use assembly lube to lubricate the idler shafts on both sides of the smart pump body.

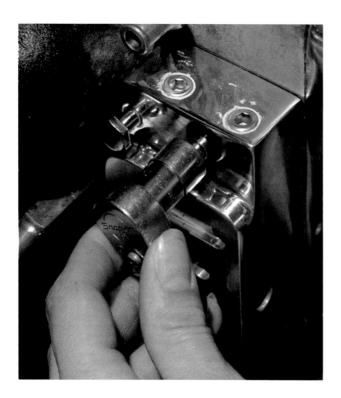

Above left: Slide the pump down the driveshaft while meshing the two return gears together. Above right: Install the new key on the driveshaft for the feed drive gear.

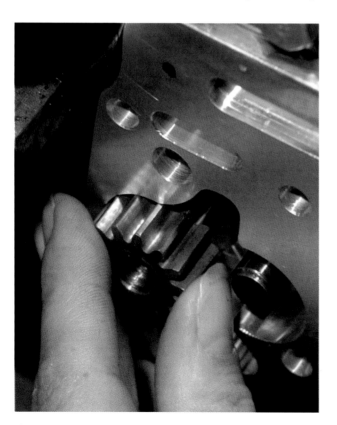

Above left: Slide the ½-inch feed drive gear (thinner of the set) on the driveshaft, making sure the key and the cutout on the gear are aligned. Above right: Install the pump idler gear onto the idle shaft in the oil pump body.

Before setting the new gasket, make sure both mating surfaces are clean. Use the four supplied Allen bolts to install the cover.

Carefully install the retaining clip on the end of the driveshaft. Have patience!

surface of oil, and install the cover and gasket using four Allen-head bolts. Torque the bolts to 110 ft-lbs. in a cross pattern. And you're done!

The TP Smart Pump is the first Evo-style pump to route motor oil to the oil filter before entering the engine. The oil is then pumped out through the oil-filter feed line, under pressure by the feed side of the pump. Once filtered, oil reenters the pump through the oil-filter return line and then lubricates the engine. The oil is then returned directly to the oil tank via the return side of the oil pump.

Some oil filters have a check valve that allows oil to flow in only one direction, this is why it is very critical that the pump is properly connected before running the engine, or serious engine damage can occur. Clean oil is now leaving the oil filter through the center. If you reverse the connections on the oil filter housing, no oil will flow through the filter. Be sure to have your service manual handy and the instructions that came with the TP pump. Improper installation of the new oil pump will void any engine warranty, and could result in severe injury or death.

Check the instructions for the listed torque specs on the bolts, and use a cross pattern to tighten.

When making the line connections, refer to the Smart Pump connections diagram that is supplied with the new pump. Oil lines running to and from the oil filter operate under high pressure and require the use of SAE J1019 ⅜-inch 400-psi WP grade hose.

Once your lines are connected according to the diagram, fill the oil tank to the listed capacity. Before firing the bike up, make sure that all the fittings and clamps are properly tightened. Connect a piece of ⅜-inch hose to the feed-line inlet fitting on the oil pump cover. TP oil pumps are not self-priming and will not gravity bleed.

You will next have to prime the oil pump. (Note: If you skip this step, it could cause severe engine damage or failure.) To prime the oil pump, you need to fill the supply-side with a squirt can. Insert the squirt can's spout into the hose and pump oil into the oil pump until resistance is felt.

Go ahead and connect the feed line from the oil tank to the oil pump. Connect the section of ⅜-inch hose to the oil-filter return fitting, insert the squirt can's spout into the hose, and pump roughly 2 to 3 ounces of oil into the engine. Doing this will lubricate the engine bearings while oil pressure is building up the first time.

Next, start the bike and let the engine run at idle speed only to build up oil pressure. If your bike has an oil pressure gauge, you'll be able to see it rise. This may take up to 25 seconds. If normal oil pressure is not reached within 25 seconds, shut off the engine and double-check all connections and lines. Do not run the engine longer than 60 seconds without oil pressure. If you are having a problem, call the oil pump manufacturer right away.

Once pressure is achieved, check your work over for any oil leaks that might have sprung up on you and take care of them. Don't ignore any leaks that you might find.

PROJECT 3 | Primary Fluid Change and Chain Adjustment

Tools Needed: Drain plug socket or wrench (on early models with hex plugs), torx or Allen socket for later models (usually T40 torx or ⅜-inch Allen), inspection fill-hole tool (normally T27 torx or 5/32- to ⅜-inch Allen). For Big Twin chain adjustments, a ⅜-inch socket and a round pry bar or Phillips screwdriver.

Time: 30 minutes **Talent:** Beginner

Cost: $10.00

Parts required: Inspection cover gasket, drain-plug O-ring, Hylomar gasket sealer, primary fluid, drain pan, shop rags

Performance Gain: Keeping your primary fluid fresh and your chain adjusted properly will prolong the life of the chain.

After the initial break-in services (if you have a brand-new bike, refer to your owner's manual for break-in procedures), you should change your transmission and primary fluids about every 5,000 miles. If you're not putting that many miles on your bike, then change these fluids at least once a year to rid them of any contaminants and condensation that may pollute the fluid.

The starting point is always, yes, the service manual. Do your research, find what parts you'll need to do the job, and purchase them. You'll be using primary fluid, transmission fluid, and an inspection cover gasket for refilling the primary fluid. Anytime you remove a gasket on your bike you will need to replace it. Never reuse a gasket. The

same applies to O-rings. This is preventative maintenance, and these items are cheap. There's no reason to invite an engine disaster by using an old gasket or o-ring that could have been replaced.

For those of you with Sportsters, the primary and tranny use the same fluid and it's called gear and chaincase lube (Bel-Ray Gear Saver 85W). The primary and tranny on Sportsters are connected, unlike Big Twins, which are separate. In the case of the Big Twins, where the compartments are separate, you can use specialty oils in both the primary and the transmission. In the primary hole, it is best to use the GL-4 transmission oil as you would in the Sportster because the wet clutch will prefer this. However, in the

Before removing the drain plug, be sure you have the tool inserted properly to prevent stripping the threads. Always have your drain pan waiting underneath the drain plug to catch the fluid.

Take the time to inspect the drain plug for excessive debris or metal shavings. This information is vital to maintaining your bike.

transmission you can now use a specialty GL-5 hypoid gear oil, which will offer additional protection in the case of sliding gear contacts, resulting in smoother shifting and quieter operation. Bel-Ray Big Twin Transmission Oil, for example, is an 85W-140 gear oil that is formulated specifically for this application. I always drain the fluids into different pans for each case.

You're not just changing the fluids during these services; this is time for you to read what your bike is trying to telling you. Inspecting fluids can find problems that you might not know are present until they cause an engine problem or, worse yet, leave you on the side of the road.

I always poke through my drained fluid. Do I see any metal chips or shavings? I look at the magnetic drain plugs

Above left: Inspecting the fluids from your bike is your opportunity to read the information your bike is giving you. Above right: To inspect the primary chain, the primary inspection cover will need to be removed.

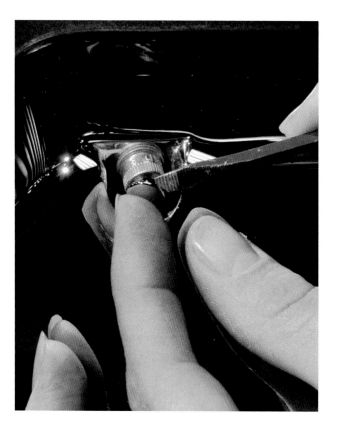

For better access to adjust the primary chain, remove the primary cover. If you have any bolt caps, these will need to be taken out first to access to the bolt heads.

Always use new gaskets wherever needed. Don't skimp and try to reuse a gasket—you'll pay in the long run with a leak.

and clean them carefully. If I see any large amount of metal, I know I need to look further than just changing the fluids because something is wrong inside my bike and I have to deal with the problem. This is my opportunity to be smart about maintaining my own bike and address the problems I find.

When changing the primary fluid, you will probably find some contaminants floating around in the pan. This is because your clutch is inside and it's a wearable item. Every time you pull that clutch in you are engaging the friction on steel discs that will slowly grind away. So unless you are seeing a huge amount of something in there, don't be freaked out by the primary fluid.

To change the primary fluid, set the drain pan underneath the primary cover. I like to take the inspection fill cover off on Sportsters before I remove the drain plug because the bolts on these covers can be a little tricky. If I can't take that fill cover off and I haven't drained the fluid yet, it's real easy to take the bike to a shop and get some help since the fluid is still in my bike. If I already drained the fluid I would have no way of being able to fill it back up if I can't get that fill cover off. So once you get that cover off, go ahead and remove the drain plug. Allow the fluid to drain completely. Look through the fluid for any contaminants (other than the normal clutch wear you might find). Next, clean the drain plug and replace any gaskets or O-rings. Use a little thread sealant and tighten the plug back to the specs in your service manual.

Above left: Use a dab of Hylomar gasket sealer to help hold the gasket in place and keep it from moving while you replace the cover. Above right: Use a ruler to measure the free play of the primary chain. Refer to your service manual for the proper amount of play and make adjustments if needed.

On big twin models, make your adjustment by turning the socket to tighten or loosen.

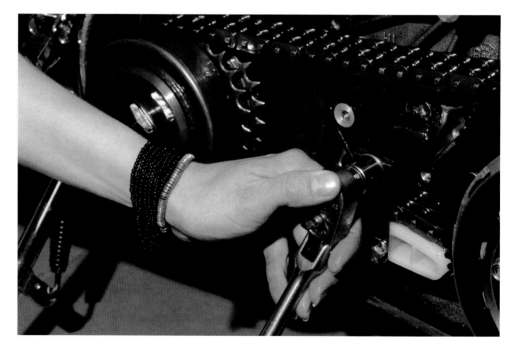

Once you've inspected your fluid, now is a good time to check the primary chain's "free play." Free play is the amount of slack in the chain, or how much it's able to flex.

Make your adjustments (see primary chain adjustment section) if needed, and refill the fluid with specified lube amounts according to your service manual. To replace the inspection cover, clean the mating surfaces and install new gaskets and the inspection cover, and tighten bolts to proper torque specs in the service manual.

A helpful tip: Do not over-tighten the drain plugs. You'll risk stripping the threads and getting stuck with a slow leaker. Replace any seals or O-rings on the plug, use a thread sealant, and make sure the plug is lined up to fit straight. Then just tighten and snug according to the service manual. I have a sign I made that hangs in my garage at the shop and reads "Do Not Over-Torque!" as a friendly reminder to myself that a good snug is all those bolts really need. Going too far will cause more damage than you

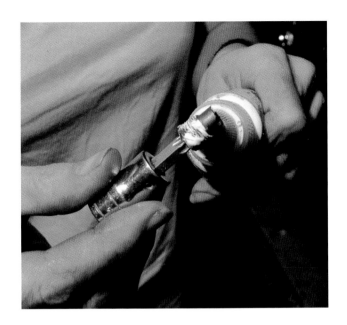

Above left: Use a thread sealant on the drain plug before re-installing it. Above right: Refill the fluid via the primary inspection cover hole. Fill it according the specs listed in your service manual.

Above left: Clean both mating surfaces of oil residue before re-installing the covers. Above right: Torque all your primary cover bolts to the listed torque specs in your service manual.

could ever want, such as the wrench-throwing scenario mentioned earlier.

When replacing gaskets, I like to use Hylomar gasket sealer. This helps hold the gasket in place and prevents it from moving. While I tighten the inspection cover back on the primary cover, the Hylomar holds the gasket in place so I can use my hands freely. It will also help in creating a better seal. Hylomar sealant, unlike silicone sealers, only dries when under clamping force. Therefore, any excess sealer getting into the oil will dissolve instead of drying into hard fragments that can clog passages or your oil pump.

Primary chain adjustment

To inspect the free play in your primary chain, you'll use your service manual to get the correct free play specifications. Checking the play in the primary chain is one of those tasks that are real easy to blow off. It's one of the simpler things to do, so I can't understand why people don't just do it. You should be checking it every time you change the primary fluid.

To adjust the chain, drain all the fluid out and remove the inspection cover, taking note of the bolt pattern. Remove the gasket and clean the surfaces. Be sure to look at the chain to see if it is well-oiled or dry. If the chain was ever run dry and becomes stiff, you'll need to replace it.

If you're checking the free play when the engine is cold, lift up on the upper half of the chain right inside the cover. The upward movement should be 5⁄8-inch to 7⁄8-inch (depending on your model, check your service manual). If you are checking the free play when the engine is warm, the movement should be no more than 3⁄8-inch to 5⁄8-inch (check for your model).

If the chain needs adjustment on Sportsters, the adjuster is at the bottom of the primary cover (see service manual). Locate the locknut and the adjusting screw. Loosen the locknut and turn the adjusting screw until the correct free play is reached. While holding the adjusting screw, go ahead and tighten the locknut according to the torque spec in the service manual.

On Big Twins, the adjuster is reached through the primary chain inspection cover. You'll locate the adjusting nut on a stud that will be loosened but not removed. This allows the adjuster to slide up to tighten and down to loosen. Make your adjustment until proper free play is achieved according to the service manual and snug the locking nut to proper torque. The Big Twin adjuster has serrated plates that mesh to firmly hold the adjusting plate from moving when the nut is re-torqued.

Replace the drain plug using thread sealant, replacing any O-rings. Refill the primary fluid to the proper amount, and be sure to use a new inspection cover gasket and torque the bolts to the spec listed in your service manual.

PROJECT 4 | Transmission Fluid Change

Tools Needed: Socket for earlier (1999 and earlier) Softail models; hex socket for later Softails, all Dynas, FLs and 4-speed models; Hex or Allen socket for dipstick/fill plug

Time: 20 minutes   **Talent:** Beginner   **Cost:** Average, $10

Parts required: Transmission oil, drain-plug O-ring, drain pan, shop rags

Performance Gain: There's no specific gain in horsepower. But changing your transmission fluid regularly is an important part of maintaining a healthy motorcycle. Your motorcycle will shift through its gears smoother and the working parts of your transmission will hold up much longer.

Next up is changing the transmission fluid. As mentioned in Project 3, a Sportster's tranny and primary share the same fluid. If you own a Sportster, you should follow the instructions in Project 3. On all other models, you'll locate your tranny's drain plug. On pre-2000 Softails, the drain is on the right side of the tranny near the dipstick. On the 2000 and later Softails, the drain is located on the bottom between the two shock absorbers. The drain plug on Dynas and FLs is located on the bottom of the transmission case next to the oil drain.

Set your drain pan under the plug and remove the drain plug. To change the transmission fluid it is best to have the bike vertical. This is where having a bike lift comes in handy. If you don't have a lift, get a friend to hold the bike upright for you. After the fluid is done draining, remember to inspect that fluid and read what it's telling you. If your fluid looks good, clean the drain plug while inspecting it as well. Replace any O-rings, use thread sealant, and snug the plug back in without over-tightening it.

To refill the fluid, the bike must also be level and upright. Refill according to spec for your model in your service manual. When checking fluid level, have bike upright and just place the dipstick back in—do not screw it all the way back on. Pull it out, check the level to make sure it's where it should be, and then screw it back into place.

See, this is what's so cool about doing the service work yourself. First, it's not that hard. You have your service manual to walk you through it all. Second, you get to read what your bike is trying to tell you.

Remove the filler plug/dipstick to drain the transmission fluid.

Remove the drain plug from underneath the chassis. On pre-1999 models, the drain plug is along the side of the transmission. On 2000 and newer models, it's located under the transmission.

Let's say there was something going on inside your tranny, maybe a gear is getting chewed up, and when you drop that fluid you'll see all the metal in your pan. No problem, you know something needs to be done. Save what you found and make an appointment to have your transmission looked at. By catching this early, you may prevent more damage from being done to other gears, the transmission shaft, shift forks, etc.

I believe that if you can ride your own bike you can do all this service work for yourself. Self-maintaining your bike is important to establish a better knowledge and understanding of your bike. You'll feel more confident when riding on the

Either have the bike level on a lift or grab a friend to hold the bike upright while the transmission fluid drains. You'll also need the bike upright to check the fluid level. When checking the fluid level, simply rest the dipstick on the threads and pull it out again. Do not screw it back in.

Remember to inspect the fluid and drain plug for unusual contaminants, and don't forget the thread sealant on the drain plug.

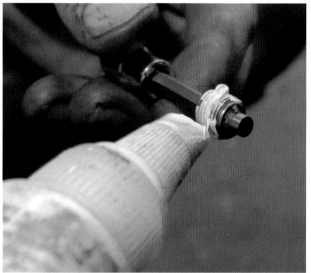

street and you'll feel better connected to your motorcycle. You take care of your body, right? You eat when you're hungry, drink when you're thirsty, and sleep when you're tired. You're doing the same for your bike.

After all, your bike is an extension of your body. You shift with your feet and adjust the throttle with your hands. You need to know the working condition of your bike like you do your body. If you have a bad back you're not going to jump down the street doing backflips are you? If your bike has bad brakes you won't be flying in and around traffic and risking having to stop suddenly.

This is why you shouldn't leave your bike sitting in your garage and then hop on for a ride without inspecting it every time you leave. You need to be prepared. You need to be in control. Servicing and maintaining your bike will put you in control.

Use a funnel to fill the fluid back to the specs listed in your service manual.

Changing the fluids is a very easy, very important, quick task to do.
I believe everyone who rides should be performing these tasks themselves.
It's important to read what your bike has to tell you.

PROJECT 5	Changing Brake Fluid

Tools Needed: A wrench to fit the brake bleeder on your caliper

Time: About two hours to change the fluid completely

Talent: Expert   **Cost:** $10.00

Parts required: Correct brake fluid for your model and a piece of clear hose to fit over the bleeder

Performance Gain: Changing your brake fluid regularly will extend the life of your brake components and keep you safer on the road.

The brake fluid in your bike, like all other fluids, needs to be changed regularly. You won't change it as often as motor oil, but you should change it every few years. It's also important to be checking the level of the brake fluid. All the information on checking the level is in your service manual.

You have two brake fluid reservoirs on your bike. One, on top of your handlebars, is your front master cylinder.

The one toward the rear of the bike, or up front by your forward controls, is the rear master cylinder.

There are a few different types of brake fluid. All newer Harley models (1972 and up) use DOT 5 fluid. Earlier models will use DOT 3, and foreign Japanese bikes will use DOT 3 or 4. You must make sure you add the correct brake fluid to your motorcycle. The information will be in your service manual.

You do not want to intermix brake fluids. I can't stress that enough. This means that you should not add DOT 3 brake fluid to a motorcycle that uses DOT 5 brake fluid. This mistake will leave you with a huge, expensive mess, not to mention no brake pressure.

I had a customer who had some "brake fluid" in his garage so he added it to his brake reservoir. The guy ended up putting the wrong brake fluid in the master cylinder. He had no brakes whatsoever and found himself having to replace all his brake lines and reseal the calipers and master cylinders. Not cheap, and not an easy job.

If you need to change your brake fluid, you'll start by fastening a hose to the bleeder screw; run the opposite end of the hose into a container filled with enough fluid to cover the end of the hose. This will prevent any air from being sucked back up in the line. Once your hose is hooked up, you can pump the brake lever or pedal to force the fluid out. Once the level in the master cylinder drops to the "add" mark, refill it with your brake fluid.

Be aware that using this method can risk pulling dirt or other contaminants through the lines and into the caliper. A longer but safer way is to use a syringe to remove fluid from the master cylinder. Be sure to clean the bottom of the reservoir of any dirt or contaminants left behind.

Once the level is back up, you will want to bleed the system to ensure that no air snuck up into the line. Bleeding brakes is probably, next to wiring, my least favorite thing to do on a bike. Refill the master cylinder with fluid and pump the lever or pedal, loosen the brake bleeder, and you'll see the old fluid fill in. Close the bleeder screw and repeat. Having an extra set of hands is helpful for pumping the lever and pedal while you work the bleeder screw.

Be sure to cover the master cylinder with a towel or hand to prevent brake fluid from oozing out, and cover painted parts on your bike. Brake fluid (especially DOT 5) is a custom painter's nightmare.

Brake fluid maintenance is not a very involved job, but if not done properly it can have serious consequences. If for any reason you don't feel confident, be sure to have a qualified mechanic do this job for you. Air in brake lines can be tricky to deal with. You may find that after a few rides your brakes need bleeding again. This is not uncommon, as air in the line can hide and not show up for a few miles.

Bleeding brakes is not necessary when just adding fluid or changing brake pads. It is only required when the hydraulic system is opened, such as removing a brake line, a caliper, or the master cylinder. Simply opening the master cylinder cap should not be cause to bleed the whole brake system.

Remove the master cylinder cover in order to inspect the level of brake fluid.

When adding to the level, be sure to use the correct brake fluid. Most later American models use a DOT 5 fluid, but check your service manual to be sure.

PROJECT 6	Changing Fork Oil

Tools Needed: Screwdriver or drain-plug tool, fork tube cap plug socket

Time: ½ hour   **Talent:** Beginner   **Cost:** $10.00

Parts required: Fork oil, fork tube plug O-ring, drain pan

Performance Gain: Like most routine maintenance jobs, this won't increase your horsepower or top speed. But good fork maintenance will keep your suspension in check, which keeps your bike handling correctly and gives you more confidence on the road.

Inside your fork tubes is an internal compression spring, a dampening rod, and fork oil. Your front suspension works first on a compression stroke, sending fork oil through the compression damping holes inside. This provides a springy but firm resistance. On the return stroke (rebound) the oil returns through the rebound holes. This is true on most models, but obviously not those with a springer front end. The holes that the fork oil travels through never change, which means the damping rates will never change either. But your fork fluid needs replacing just like all the fluids on your bike. As this fluid breaks down, so does its ability to provide that damping resistance.

Using different weights of fork fluids will affect the rate of speed the oil passes through the holes. A heavier fluid will allow the oil to pass more slowly, and vice versa for a lighter fluid. Other than upgrading the springs and changing from the damping rod fork to a Gold Valve Cartridge emulator, there really isn't much you can do to enhance the performance of your stock front-end suspension. But changing the fluid regularly will sustain that level of performance.

Above left: Loosen the drain screw on the lower leg of your front end to allow the fork oil to drain. Don't forget to set your drain pan underneath. Above right: Once your bike is lifted and there is no load on the front end, remove the fork cap plugs. Use caution on this step because the springs are under pressure. Wear eye protection, and cover any painted parts that could be damaged from flying fork caps.

Allow all of the fluid to drain completely into the drain pan.

Here's one of the motorcycle specialty tools I mentioned earlier. A fork cap socket makes the job easier.

If you are making performance upgrades to your engine, you'll want to upgrade the suspension as well as the braking system to handle the horsepower increase. Understand that improving the performance of one system on your bike will require you to improve all other systems to compensate.

Before you get started on upgrading your suspension, however, you should learn how to replace the fluid in your stock forks. Of course, have your manual out to help walk you through this job.

Remove the fork drain screw and washer from the bottom of one slider (lower leg). Let the fluid drain. You can compress the front suspension to help this along. If the fluid looks light brown or emulsified, it means that it has been contaminated by water and you'll want to replace the fork seals. Go ahead and drain the other side.

Use a can of brake cleaner to remove old oil residue from the bottom of your forks, and place a drain pan underneath to catch run off.

Lift the bike so the front wheel is off the ground, this will ensure the spring is not under a load. If you do not do this step and attempt to remove the fork-tube caps, the tension could cause the caps and springs to fly out.

Check your service manual for exact fluid fill specs. Note the different amounts for a wet fork and a dry fork. A dry fork is when the front end is completely disassembled. If you're just changing the fluid, it's considered a wet fork.

Use a small funnel to fill the fluid back into the fork.

Above left: As with any gaskets, the O-rings on the fork caps will need replacing when you're changing the fork oil. Above right: Of course you'll remember to tighten up the fork drain screws prior to refilling the fork, right? When you're done, carefully replace the fork plug caps.

Once the load is off the front end, remove the fork-tube cap and O-rings carefully—these springs are still under pressure.

Replace the drain screw and washer on the leg prior to adding fresh fluid. Your service manual will list the specified amount of fork fluid to refill with. Make note that the service manual will have two different amounts listed. One will be for a dry fork, which would be if you completely dis-sembled the front end, cleaned, and reassembled it. The other amount is for a wet fork, which is exactly what you have. You're simply draining the fork oil and refilling. Replace the fork tube cap O-rings and tighten to spec.

PROJECT 7	Lubing and Adjusting Cables

Tools Needed: Cable lube tool (optional), open-ended wrenches (½-inch or ⁹⁄₁₆-inch)

Time: 20 minutes to an hour   **Talent:** Beginner (throttle), intermediate (clutch)

Cost: Only a few bucks, and one can will probably last as long as your bike.

Parts required: Cable lube

Performance Gain: Again, this won't boost your motorcycle's power or speed, but it will keep your throttle and clutch cables from getting stiff. It makes for a smoother ride with less chance of cable failure on the road.

If you're like me, when you ride you probably love to grab the throttle and slowly give it a twist, feeling the engine start to pull you. I'd say that's the number- one reason why I love to ride. The feeling of slowly rolling the throttle on is pure fun. You want that throttle to respond to your hand precisely.

Checking for proper throttle response is an important part of inspecting your motorcycle. Throttle failure could put you in a bad place. Twist the throttle to make sure it moves freely without binding. Any sticking or slow return needs attention to either cables or inside the switch housing where the cables connect to the grip.

If your clutch cable needs replacing on FXST-style Big Twins, you'll remove the trans-end cover. Your service manual will point out where to change it on your model.

Using your service manual, you'll see a mileage interval of when to lube your cables. I lube the lever pivots as well.

In order to lube the cables, I recommend you use a cable-lubricating tool made by Motion Pro. On the throttle and idle cables, you'll back off the adjuster, pull as much cable out as you can, install the lubricating tool, and lube away.

I perform this next service check with my bike running. Turn the handlebars a full turn left and right to see if the idle changes. If it does, then you'll need to have the cables adjusted. Reset your throttle adjustment in the cable at the adjusters. If you remove your handlebar housings and expose the barrels on the cable ends that fit into your grips' grooves, make sure they are lined up properly and use a little anti-seize compound on them to secure position.

Clutch cable

To lube the clutch cable, begin by backing off the inline adjuster completely. Remove the eyelet from the clutch lever, place your cable lubing tool on the end, and lube away. It's a good idea to lube the cable above and below the adjuster. Use some anti-seize compound on the eyelet and replace the cable end back into the lever. It's a good idea to place a small amount of anti-seize compound on your cable adjuster as well.

The clutch cable is a little more involved to adjust. If you feel the clutch slipping when releasing the lever, you should have your clutch adjusted. In order to adjust the clutch cable, you need two wrenches to take up the slack in the cable up at the lever. Loosen the locknut on the adjuster

Be sure to remove all of the old gasket from the surfaces. A single-edge razor works best for gasket removal.

You will need to clean old oil residue from the transmission side cover. A parts cleaner works best for this messy job.

Thread the clutch cable (use thread sealant on the end) back into the transmission side cover by spinning the cover around the cable.

Dab a little grease on the ball bearing ramp and replace the bearings.

Above left: Connect the clutch cable into the release lever and replace it. Above right: A pair of snap-ring pliers is needed to set the snap ring back in place. Use caution on this step, and make sure you have eye protection on. A snap ring can fly very far.

With the new gasket in place, carefully replace the transmission side cover and torque the bolts to listed specs in your service manual.

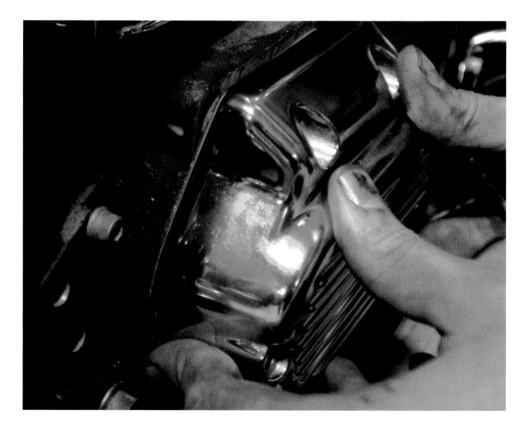

It's a good idea to lube the cables where they connect to the throttle sleeve under the switch housing.

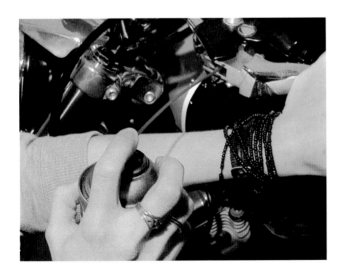

When lubing the cables, lube the pivot on the lever as well.

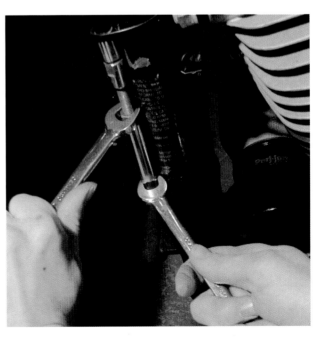

Two open-end wrenches are needed for an inline clutch cable adjustment.

A spray sealant can also be used on gaskets. Coat each side evenly and be sure to lay the gasket down on a clean surface.

sleeve until you have about ⅟₁₆-inch free play at the cable. Once this is achieved go ahead and tighten.

This is a pretty straightforward job, but it can be a little touchy. If you don't feel confident you should leave this job to a mechanic. The clutch is what controls power, and power and braking are the two things we want in the best working condition we can possibly have.

The clutch on your bike is made up of friction and steel plates along with a spring plate. The friction plates are mated to the clutch shell, which gets powered by the engine through the primary chain. The steel plates and spring plate are mated to the clutch hub, which moves the rear wheel through the transmission and final drive belt or chain. So

you can see how important that clutch is and why you want to inspect it to make sure it's working properly.

A lot of times the spring plate inside the clutch (made up of two plates riveted together) will wear itself apart. The rivets will end up at the bottom of your clutch basket housing and cause clutch problems, slippage, and damage. The clutch will not fully disengage or release as well. You should be looking for signs like this when changing the primary fluid.

If the spring plate in your bike does come apart, I recommend upgrading to the Barnett extra-plate clutch kit available at any motorcycle shop, dealer, or aftermarket supplier. This kit replaces that spring-riveted plate with an extra clutch plate.

CHAPTER 4
SERVICE INTERVALS

The really cool thing about the service manual is the fact that it has a built-in schedule of routine maintenance for you to follow at certain mileage intervals. This is totally cool; you don't have to remember this stuff because it's right there for you in an easy-to-read chart form.

The chart will show the odometer reading and every task listed for the service you need to perform at that certain mileage. You will see letters indicating what you should do for that listed task: "I" is for inspect, "R" for replace, "L" for lubricate, "T" for tighten or check for proper torque, and an "X" meaning you should perform a specific task.

You'll also find a diagram of your bike pointing out where everything is. Even the obvious parts like the fuel tank and oil tank are mapped out.

Something else you should pay attention to is the OEM number listed next to each part. This stands for original equipment manufacturer. You can jot this number down and refer to it when ordering your parts.

Along with your service manual, you should also purchase a factory parts catalog. A parts catalog is nice because it has exploded drawings of everything with easy-to-locate part numbers for everything on your bike. I'm talking part

A FEW THINGS TO JOT DOWN:

The size of your spark plugs: Make a note that different manufacturers of the same size plug might have a different-sized hex, meaning the wrench you'll use to install a new plug might be different from the wrench you used to remove the old one, even though the size is the same.

Your tire sizes: Write down all the details of your tires, including the brand, the width, the tire type, and the amount of air each one holds. Your front and back tires can vary widely in size and pressure.

The size of your wheels: Your wheels may be of different diameters or widths. Wheel size (and type) will be important when working on forks, brakes, rear suspension, final drive, fender replacement—the list is endless.

Fuel-tank capacity: It's good to know this when planning gas stops on long rides and to help in calculating fuel mileage. Remember, your bike tells you how it's running when you perform routine maintenance. A surefire way to know something's wrong is when your fuel mileage takes a significant drop.

The make, year, and model of your bike: As mentioned earlier, you'd be surprised how many people don't know the basic details. Keep in mind that some used motorcycles have mix-and-match parts. Write down everything you know about your motorcycle.

You can keep a journal of this information on your bike in your saddlebag or tool pouch for quick reference. It won't be long before this info is just embedded in your head and you won't need any lists. Trust me, once you start taking control of working on your bike this info will be second nature.

Along with this information, make yourself a service interval chart to keep track of everything you do to your bike. Most newer models come with a great checklist toward the back of the owner's manual. This will help to remind you what you've done, when you've done it, what needs to be done, and when it has to be done again. Keeping track of all your service work also helps when it's time to sell your bike. A potential buyer will feel more confident about the bike seeing a visual chart of all the services performed at the appropriate mileage intervals.

numbers from fenders and gas tanks to the tiniest of circlips and filler caps. All parts salespeople have a reference to OEM numbers and can cross-reference to find your exact part. I like to have this info on hand so I know for sure I'm getting the right part I need, rather than relying on a parts salesperson looking it up for me.

I've made mistakes ordering parts or looking up parts for customers. Mistakes can happen, and human error will always be present. But if you don't look up the part yourself, you only have yourself to blame.

Remember, servicing your bike is all about preventative maintenance. This means that everything from performing inspections, changes, adjustments, and using correct parts can lower your odds of mechanical failure at the most inconvenient time.

Looking at your service manual you'll find the routine maintenance and servicing mapped out at certain mileage intervals. This is the way your manufacturer prefers to see its motorcycles serviced. If your motorcycle is still under warranty, this schedule is often important for you to continue coverage. It's also important when considering resale value. If you're able to tell a prospective buyer that you've followed the manufacturer's recommendation to the letter, and the motorcycle shows that you've taken care of it, you'll have a much easier time selling it for a good price.

Services are generally performed every 2,500 miles (light), 5,000 miles (medium), and 10,000 miles (heavy). Everyone puts a different amount of miles on his or her bike, due to climate, landscape, and lifestyle. For instance, I never get to ride anymore now that I'm running my shop. I'm lucky if I put on 2,500 miles in a year. So it could take me four years to reach 10,000 miles in order to perform that level of service.

Well, we all know it's not a good idea to go that long without performing certain services. This is where you need to customize the service of your bike to your riding style. I make it a point to perform a 10,000-mile service on my bike once a year even if I'm not getting the actual miles on it.

How about the extreme opposite situation? Let's say your motorcycle is your primary ride and you ride it a lot—30,000-plus miles a year. Well, that rider will have to adjust the service intervals to suit the mileage that bike is getting and perform these tasks a little more often.

You'll be able to work out service intervals that suit you best, but let me share with you how I handle the servicing of my bike. I usually wait until the winter months to do the more involved work (10,000-mile service) on my bike. I live in Pittsburgh, so winter leaves me with six months to get this all done. When my bike is ready for a tire and I notice my brake pads are looking the slightest bit worn, I just go ahead and change them. I look at it this way, I already have the caliper off the bike, so half the work is done. Every time I change a tire I pull my wheel bearings off, inspect them, and repack them if they need it. I always replace the wheel seals too because this is such a low-cost, easy way to keep my bearings free from debris. Again, the wheel is already off the bike and half the work is done.

Changing the oil and fluids (Chapter 3) is not expensive and it's the best thing you can do to prolong the life of your bike. Don't be afraid to over-service your bike. The more you touch your bike, whether you're cleaning or servicing, you are forced to physically be in contact with your bike and you will increase the odds of finding something that needs attention.

There are plenty of options for spark plugs. Try a few brands and find one you like.

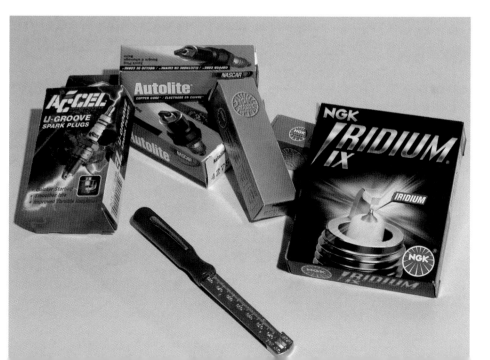

<table>
<tr><td>

PROJECT 8

</td><td>

Reading and Changing Spark Plugs

</td></tr>
</table>

Tools Needed: Socket or wrench to fit plug

Time: 10 minutes

Talent: Beginner

Cost: Average price for a set of plugs is $6

Parts required: New spark plugs

Performance Gain: Reliable spark plugs make your engine run at optimum capacity. More important, inspecting your plugs can tell you a lot about how the engine is running.

Spark plugs, not much to them in physical appearance but they hold so much power for the operation of your bike. Spark plugs are responsible for transferring energy from the ignition system into the combustion chamber. Spark plugs also transfer heat into the cylinder head where it is pulled away via the exhaust stroke. Why do you think those exhaust pipes are so hot?

Your engine mixes fuel with air and combustion happens when the air-fuel mixture meets the spark from the spark plug. The faster you get air and fuel in, and the quicker you get the exhaust out, the more performance of your bike will be enhanced, but that's a whole other subject.

Plugs come in different heat range settings. Which is best for you? Well, nine times out of ten, the heat range

Above left: To change the spark plugs, you'll start by removing the spark plug wires from the plugs. Above right: Use an open-end wrench or socket to break the spark plug loose from the cylinder head.

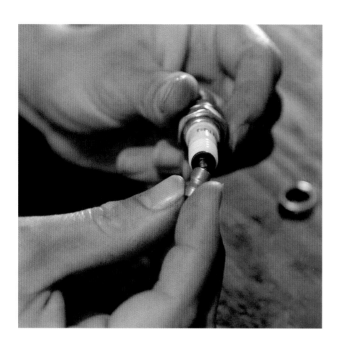

Spark plugs come with the center electrode tip and sealing washer separate from the plug. These will need to be assembled before installing the plug into the cylinder head.

recommended in your service manual will be right for you. If you were loading up a dresser or doing some real hard touring in high temps you might want to consider using a colder running plug, vice versa for the opposite situation. Before going against your manufacturer's recommendation, however, tell your local mechanic or dealership what you'll be doing on the bike and ask his or her opinion.

As you start with the plugs, keep in mind that, like the fluids in your bike, you're not just changing them—this is your chance to read what your bike is telling you.

You'll need to determine what size hex your plugs are mounted with and then grab the correct socket to match so you can remove the plugs. Wait until your bike has cooled before you change the plugs. Remove the plug wires from the

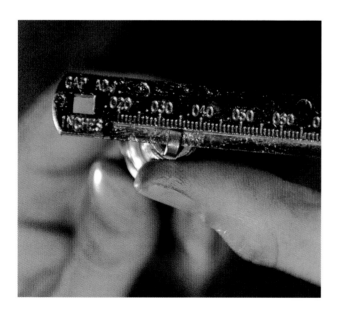

Above left: Be sure to use a quality gapping tool to set the spark plug gap according to your service manual. Above right: Here you can see the difference in the color of two spark plugs. Refer to your service manual for plug diagnosing.

spark plug and go ahead with your wrench or ratchet and break the spark plug loose. Once you loosen the plug enough you can grab it with your hand and remove it.

Spark plugs should have a beige color to them. If they look real black or white and you can't pinpoint why, then you'll want to have a certified mechanic take a look. Your spark plugs should also be the same color. You never want to see one spark plug black and one beige. A fuel mixture problem could be robbing you of power.

If the plugs are totally black and smell of fuel, then the bike is running rich. This means it's getting too much fuel during the process of mixing fuel with air. A black plug could also mean your air filter is clogged or maybe you made a change to your bike, like a new set of pipes, which is affecting how fast the exhaust is being pulled away, or it could be as simple as a change in altitude and temperature. A rich plug will get clogged with carbon and unspent fuel and you will lose power as the plug tip temperature drops and causes the plug to foul out.

If the plugs are totally white, then the bike is telling you it's not getting enough fuel and it's running lean. This bleached look will indicate the cylinder and plug-tip temperatures are running high.

When changing spark plugs, you'll need to gap the space between the ground electrode and the center electrode according to the spec listed in your service manual. In other words, the space between the little curved piece of metal and the tip of the plug. Use a spark plug gapping tool to get the correct gap. The wrong gap on a spark plug can cause your engine to run improperly.

I recommend cleaning the threads on the cylinder head before installing a new plug to rid any dirt that may have collected there. Refer to your service manual for the proper torque on the plug. Don't over-tighten when installing the spark plug back into the cylinder head or you'll be rather annoyed when you want to replace that spark plug and can't break it loose.

I love changing spark plugs. It's one of the first things I learned how to do to my bike. Spark plugs give you so much information about how your bike is performing. It takes years of experience to read a plug properly and make changes according to the look of the plug, but if you decide down the road that you want to make some changes to your bike, maybe a new air cleaner or exhaust, you will have to pull those spark plugs and inspect them to see if the changes you made are affecting the performance of your bike. In situations like these, get some help from someone with more experience or from a qualified mechanic who can read a plug and diagnose what to do next.

PROJECT 9	Aftermarket Spark Plug Wires

Tools Needed: Your hands

Time: 10 minutes   **Talent:** Beginner   **Cost:** $25–$40

Parts required: New spark plug wires, dielectric grease

Performance Gain: Better spark delivery from the ignition system to the plug means more consistent power.

Spark plug wires are a very important part of the ignition system on your bike. A set of bad spark plug wires can have too much resistance making it hard for the voltage to reach the plug, causing a weak spark. The wires could have bad insulation and cause a misfire. If the wires absorb moisture, they can cause problems when it's raining or if it's damp.

Check your plug wires for any worn areas or signs of cracks. If you see anything that looks iffy, you'll want to replace the plug wires.

Plug wires are sold in all sorts of colors and are sized to fit your model of bike, giving you a custom "cut-to-fit" wire kit.

Changing wires is very simple: Remove the plug wires from the spark plugs and the coil. Next, go ahead and replace them with the new wires the same way they came off.

I recommend Taylor, Accell, or Crane. These wires use a stronger material for the insulation, which will better deliver the high-voltage current to the plug.

A new plug wire compared to an old corroded wire—if your wires look like this, replace them.

Place a dab of dielectric grease into the plug boot. This will seal out moisture to prevent corrosion.

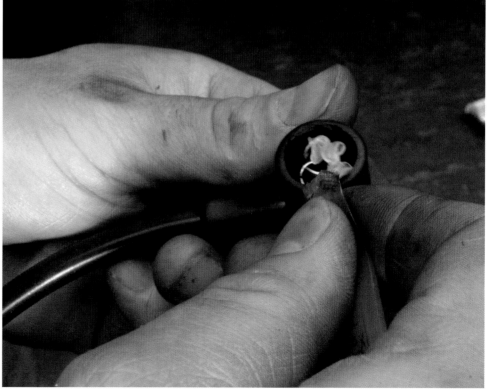

Remove the old plug wires and replace them with the new sets at the coil.

PROJECT 10 | Air Filter Cleaning and Changing

Tools Needed: Phillips screwdriver or Allen socket (Note: Some bolt on with a torx bolt.)

Time: 30 minutes   **Talent:** Beginner

Cost: Lifetime filter: $60–$80. Paper element: $20–$40

Parts required: If replacing, new air filter. If cleaning, air filter cleaner and air filter oil. Shop towels.

Performance Gain: Less restriction on air delivery to the engine.

When the service chart says it's time to inspect your air filter, you'll start by taking the air cleaner cover off. The air cleaner is usually held on by two Phillips screws.

Once the air cleaner cover is off, remove the old or dirty filter. If using a cleanable filter, you'll spray on the air filter cleaner and wash off with water. Let this air dry in the sun. Never try to blow the filter dry with a compressor as this can damage the pleats. When the filter is dry, go ahead and re-oil with the air filter oil. If you are replacing the paper filter with a lifetime filter, it will be oiled and ready to go out of the box.

Once my stock air filter was dirty and ready to be replaced I switched to a lifetime high-flow filter, like those made by K&N or Green. The filter will flow the air faster, which helps in the fuel-air mixing process. I also use a performance lifetime air filter because I'll never have to buy

Before accessing the air filter, you need to remove the air cleaner cover. Each model uses different hardware. This model requires a Philips screwdriver.

Once the cover is off, go ahead and remove the air filter element. Here I have a reusable K&N element I will be cleaning rather than replacing.

Remove any oil or debris from the backing plate and back side of the element.

For lifetime filters, use the specified filter cleaner to maintain the filter element. Just spray the cleaner into the pleats of the element.

Once the filter is sprayed with the required cleaner, wash it off with water. Let the filter sit in the sun for a while to dry out the water. Never use an air gun to dry it off.

Once the filter is dried, use the required filter oil and re-oil the filter before putting it back in the air cleaner. This K&N filter will last me a lifetime.

another one. The new air filter is simply serviced, cleaned, and re-oiled. Every 2,500 miles or so I'll take the filter out and use an air filter cleaner then re-oil the air filter before putting it back in the air cleaner.

You want your bike to do two things as best as it can. Go and stop. You want to be able to throttle and get out of the way of potential hazards if needed, and stop on a dime if you have to avoid something dangerous in your way.

Let's say you're behind the Griswold family on vacation on a busy road. You see an obvious potential for one of the kids' bikes or a suitcase to come flying off and hit you on your bike. When I see a car packed like that in front of me on the highway, I crack the throttle and pass when it's safe to do so.

If my bike wasn't in top running performance, I might not be able to get up and go when I twist the throttle. I could get poor throttle response and hesitation before the power kicks in to the rear wheel. It's important for me to know the working condition of my bike for dangerous situations and for the satisfaction of knowing I'm in control.

A clean air filter will keep your bike running as smooth as it should. A clogged air filter will rob you of power and fuel mileage.

Tighten the cover back up on the air cleaner to the torque specs listed in your service manual.

PROJECT 11 | Brake Pad Change

Tools Needed: Flat screwdriver or clamp, Allen or torx wrench (later models, 12-point ¼-inch socket)

Time: 15 to 30 minutes   **Talent:** Intermediate

Cost: Depending on the compound you choose, $20–$50

Parts required: Brake pads

Performance Gain: You'll be able to stop more effectively and safely.

The most important thing you want to be able to do as best as you can on your motorcycle is stopping. You'll find yourself having to stop real fast probably more often then you'd like, or you'll be eating the bumper of the guy in front of you who decided to hit the brakes at the last damn minute.

Looking over your brake pads is the easiest preventative maintenance you can do. First, you need to know that, as with any part, you have more options than simply stock replacement. When it's time to replace your brake pads, which pads should you use? This is another one of those questions I'm asked daily.

In order to answer this question, let's get some basics down about brake pad compounds. There are a few different compounds of pads to choose from. In order to know which will be best for you, answer some questions honestly. What type of riding do you do? Are you a real aggressive rider, cutting it up on the street and pulling a fist full of throttle to pull you through the turns and then grabbing the brake hard for sudden stops? Do you ride low-key and cruise your bike around town? Are you riding a fully loaded bike cross-country? Is your engine hopped up with big horsepower gains? These questions need to be answered before you can decide what type of brake compound will suit you best.

Here are two brake pads of different compounds. The left is a sintered pad and the right is an organic.

Use a flathead screwdriver or small pry bar to push the piston back in. This will make room to get the pads out.

Another question you'll need to answer is what type of rotors are you using? Are you using stock zinc rotors? Did you upgrade your rotors to a floating or stainless rotor? Again, certain compounds suit rotors differently.

Basically, you have three sets of pads to choose from. Sintered brake pads are usually referred to as metallic pads. Sintered pads are made up of ground metals: copper alloy, graphite, and other materials. Sintered pads have great stopping ability under most riding conditions and work well when wet. Sintered pads are great for stainless rotors in that they eliminate squealing and galling like some organic pads do. You probably won't get as many miles out of them, however, since they create and generate more heat, they might wear your rotor a little faster.

Left: Once you've gained the clearance, remove the pads one at a time. Above: If you're not sure if your brake pads need changing, compare them to a new set of pads. Here is an old pad (left) next to a new one.

Organic pads are made up of resin and fibers. Asbestos was once used, but Kevlar has since replaced that material. Semi-metallic pads are organic pads with small bits of metal throughout. Generally, organic pads are softer and easier on rotors but you won't have the strong grabbing power a sintered pad will give you. Organic pads wear faster and may not have as much grab when hot. You also take the risk of organic pads glazing over.

Ceramic compounds are also available. They are very resilient to heat and are basically suited for race applications. You can get some brake pads that have ceramic material throughout for street use.

As I mentioned above, answer the questions first, consider the rotor, caliper, and your riding style before you decide what compound you want to try. Another suggestion is to talk with your local mechanic or motorcycle dealer and ask for their recommendation.

The next question is what brand you should use. For Harley-Davidsons, the leading aftermarket brake manufactures to choose from are Ferodo, EBC, SBS, Dunlop, and Vesrah. Which is best? That is going to be up to you. I recommend trying them all until you find one you're really happy with. Trust me, you'll know what feels good. In my experience of trying different brands I've been real happy with Ferodo.

If you're riding your bike with the stock caliper, rotors, and pads and don't feel as though you could be stopping any better, then maybe staying with that stock setup is right for you. You have to be the one making these decisions. It's your bike, your riding style, and your choice.

You'll need to be able to see your brake pads sitting in your brake caliper. If you have saddlebags, this is where they become a pain.

Your bike has a fully hydraulic brake system. The front brake is on your handlebar control assembly. It consists of the brake lever and the front master cylinder or reservoir; this holds the brake fluid for the front caliper.

The rear brake is part of your foot controls. This consists of the brake pedal and a rear master cylinder or reservoir that holds the brake fluid for the rear brake caliper. You'll be checking brake fluid levels in each master cylinder about every 5,000 miles. Again this is in your service manual.

You don't have to remove the brake caliper from the bike in order to inspect pad thickness; you can see the thickness by looking down into the caliper. If you have any doubts, then remove the caliper to get a good look.

Alright, first things first . . . that's right, go get your service manual. Look over and inspect the brake pads every 2,500 miles (see your chart in the service manual). When changing tires, if your brake pads look remotely worn go

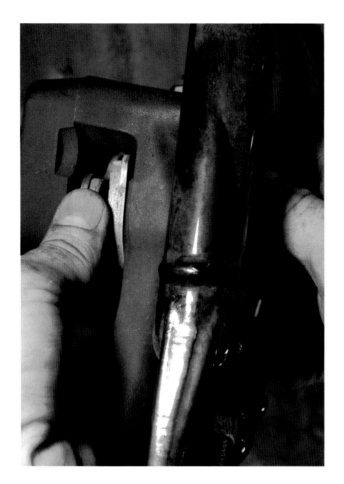

Place the new brake pads into the caliper, positioned properly and lined up with the pin. Then tighten the pin.

Put the caliper back on the bike. A convenient time to do this job is during a tire change.

ahead and replace them; half the job is done since we have the caliper off the wheel. You'll need to replace the brake pads if they are worn down to ⅟₁₆ inch (1.6 mm) or less. If you're not sure what the thickness should look like, compare them to a set of new brake pads.

Once the caliper is off the bike, you'll need to remove the brake pads. It's easier to do them one at a time. In order to gain a little access room, gently pry the piston back with a screwdriver or small pry bar. Place a shop rag over any sharp edges of the tool to prevent any gouging if the tool slips.

When the new pads are in place and the caliper is back on the bike, pump the brake to regain pressure. With new brake pads, allow a break-in time and be gentle when using the brakes for a few miles.

If you don't feel comfortable doing it yourself, make an appointment with your certified mechanic to have the pads changed or have someone with extensive knowledge show you how. Changing brake pads is a pretty straightforward job, but if done wrong the consequences can be fatal.

Remember, we need our bikes to do two things as best as they can. Throttle and stop.

PROJECT 12 | Rotor Upgrade

Tools Needed: Torx bit; axle nut socket; pliers; wrench or socket for pinch bolts or clamp; hand torch; Allen, torx, or socket for caliper removal

Time: 45 minutes per whee   **Talent:** Experienced   **Cost:** $100–$350, depending on the rotor

Parts required: New rotor, new hardware, blue Locktite

Performance Gain: You'll enhance the performance of the brake system.

When inspecting rotors, look for any deep wear and measure the rotor for proper thickness. If you have a measuring caliper, you can measure the thickness yourself. The proper measurement is stamped on the side of the rotor.

If while inspecting your rotors you see a visual warp, this is the perfect time to upgrade to a more performance-geared rotor. If you have made a power increase to your bike, you'll need to compensate for this by upgrading your braking system.

If you have decided to upgrade your rotors, what do you upgrade to? Fixed or floating? I'll give you the lowdown on the two. Let's start with the fixed rotor. The fixed rotor mounts solidly to the wheel hub. When a rotor heats up from friction via the brake pads it wants to move. We all know things expand and shift when hot. Since the outer area where the pads touch gets hotter than the inner surface, the rotor won't be able to expand since it's mounted solidly to the hub. A floating rotor is made up of two components: the inner surface, which is mounted solidly to the wheel hub, and the outer disc (the surface the pads touch), which is mounted by rivets to the inner piece. With the pad track area mounted to the inner area, the rotor can move freely when hot. This free movement creates much more room for expansion and leaves less room for warping.

If you were to come into my shop and ask my opinion, I'd tell you to upgrade to floating rotors. Floating rotors self-center in the caliper, which helps reduce friction loss. The overall lighter weight of a floating rotor equals less rotational mass.

I was working on a Softail with a warped rotor, so I decided to upgrade the discs to a set of Ferodo floating rotors. This bike also had sufficient engine work resulting in horsepower increases, so it was time to bump up the braking system to match the engine. Since money obviously plays a role in what parts we put on our bikes and when we can put them on, we decided to start with the rotors knowing in the near future we will be upgrading the calipers. Remember, when upgrading one system on your bike you'll need to upgrade others to compensate for the change.

First things first, have your service manual opened to the rotor section. You'll need to lift the bike in order to take the wheels off. Make sure you have it tied down securely before lifting. Once you have the wheel off, lay it down on something soft and clean. Carpet remnants work great for this.

When removing the rotor bolts, you will more than likely run into stubborn bolts that will not want to budge for you,

Floating rotors are the way to go when updating your brakes.

When dealing with stubborn rotor bolts, a handheld torch will loosen up old Loctite. Be sure to take your time with rotor bolts. A stripped out rotor bolt is a major pain to deal with.

this is from the Locktite. Take a bottle torch and warm the bolts up enough to loosen the Locktite. Be patient with this step; you don't want to strip the bolts out. On a weekly basis I have wheels brought in to the shop by customers with rotor bolts stripped out. When it gets to that point, your only option is to try drilling the bolt out or welding a nut on the bolt. So take your time, go slow, and use some heat on the bolts if necessary. If you're in a no-win situation, take the wheel to a shop and let a mechanic remove them for you.

When the old rotor is off, place the new rotor on the hub and use new rotor hardware. It's strongly recommended to use new hardware. If you have to reuse the old rotor bolts (assuming you didn't strip the bolts out when removing them), clean the threads thoroughly with a wire brush and use a fresh drop of blue Locktite. Tighten the bolts to the torque spec listed in your service manual using a cross pattern.

Go ahead and install the wheel back on the bike as well as the caliper. Refer to the service manual again for the recommended axle torque specifications. Spin the wheel to ensure free travel with no hang-ups.

Once the wheel is spinning freely, apply the brake to ensure proper stopping.

Above: Here you can see the damage excess heat will do to a rotor. This is an extreme case of warping. Left: Always use new hardware when upgrading the rotors on your bike.

Place a small amount of blue Loctite on the new rotor hardware. A small dab goes a long way.

Torque the rotor bolts with a torque wrench to the specs listed in your service manual.

PROJECT 13 | Caliper Upgrade (Performance Machine)

Tools Needed: Line wrench, ¼-inch socket to remove rear axle, Allen or torx sockets to remove caliper mounting bolts, torque wrench

Time: 2 to 3 hours (depending on cooperation of brakes when bleeding the line)

Talent: Expert   **Cost:** About $400–$500

Parts required: New calipers, brake banjo bolts (if needed), caliper shims included in new caliper kit, new cotter pin for rear axle

Performance Gain: This is a braking system upgrade. You'll increase your stopping ability and lower the heat friction on your rotors.

Increase your stopping power by upgrading your calipers.

As stated earlier, we want our bikes to do two things as best as they can: Throttle and stop. The stock braking system on Harley-Davidsons is fine for the stock engine displacement, but let's be honest, who keeps their engine stock? We all upgrade the performance of our bikes: pipes, suspension, air cleaner, carb, cam work, headwork. I can go on and on. A simple upgrade like the S&S easy setup kit, which consists of slip-on mufflers, CV carb jets, and an air cleaner, will increase your horsepower by ten. Any horsepower gain will alter the balance between your braking ability and engine performance.

Once you increase the power of your engine, you are putting a significant increase of heat on the braking surface.

Stock braking systems can only dissipate a certain amount of heat before they lose effectiveness. There are a few ways we can reduce the heat on our braking systems: change rotors, increase rotor size using floating rotors, change brake pad compounds, and increase the amount of pistons in our calipers.

One- and two-piston calipers contain all the stopping pressure in a small area on the rotor, which creates hot spots. A four- or a six-piston caliper will dissipate the pressure on the rotor over a larger area reducing heat and increasing stopping power. Better yet is a differential bore caliper. A race-inspired technology designed to compensate for excessive pad wear at the entry point of the disc, the dif-

93

Start by removing the caliper mounting bolts.

Here is a close-up of the stock single-piston caliper.

You don't want to disconnect the brake line until you are ready to connect it to the new caliper. You can let the caliper hang loose and out of the way while you work.

ferential bore caliper uses a smaller piston at the disc entry and a larger piston at the exit. The pad-to-rotor contact is much more efficient in increasing braking power without increasing heat.

When we upgrade brake pads, rotors, and calipers, it's also important not to overlook the brake lines and master cylinder. After all, these are integral parts of the braking system. How about those stock brake lines? Stock rubber brake lines allow themselves to expand when pressurized with brake fluid. The total pressure is not being used to move the pistons in the caliper since a portion is now being used to expand the rubber line. Upgrading to a braided steel line will reduce expansion.

If you do upgrade your braking system, however, be sure the master cylinder bore is still adequate enough to move the fluid properly.

You can see the brake pads sitting in the bracket now that the caliper has been removed.

Before starting your caliper upgrade, take a moment to make sure the new parts are correct for your model.

Before we start, have your service manual in hand. You'll need to pay close attention to the caliper centering over the brake rotor. These calipers use DOT 5 brake fluid. If you are not upgrading the brake line at this time, you will simply be switching the line over at the banjo fitting. Do not disconnect the old caliper from the brake line until the new caliper is in place and you're ready to bleed the system. This way you won't lose as much brake fluid.

We chose Performance Machine (PM) calipers for this 1996 XL. This caliper kit was designed to fit this year and model. It's always best to make sure the calipers are correct before starting the project. Start by lifting the bike high enough to remove the rear wheel. Make sure the bike is tied down securely to the lift.

To install the rear caliper, first remove the rear wheel by taking the cotter pin out, sliding the rear axle out, and

Set the new caliper bracket onto
the swingarm. Be sure the axle
hole on the bracket is lined up
with the axle adjuster.

The front caliper on this model
gets mounted directly to the front
end. No bracket is needed.

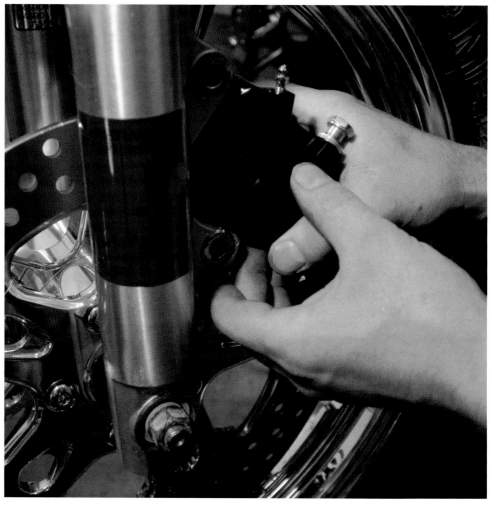

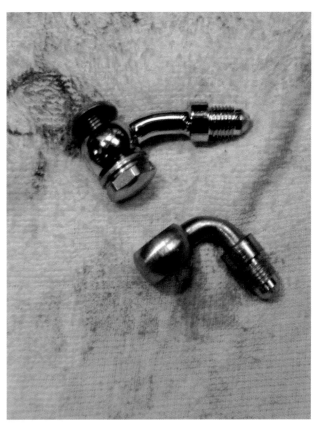

Above: Line up the mounting bolts on the caliper bracket, and set the rear caliper in the bracket. Above right: I had to change the degree of bend on the banjo bolt for brake line clearance on my front caliper. Notice the difference of degree in the bend from 90 to 35. Sometimes that's all it takes.

Thread the banjo bolt into the caliper just before connecting the brake line.

Use a wrench to tighten the brake line onto the banjo bolt.

You must torque the caliper to the torque specs listed in your service manual.

Remove the master cylinder cover before bleeding the system. This is where you will add the brake fluid.

Use a line wrench on the bleeder valve to bleed the brake system. A section of hose is used to allow the air and fluid to flow out.

Top off the master cylinder to the fill line using the correct brake fluid for your model.

An extra set of hands will help with bleeding the system, especially to pump the pedal while you work the bleeder valve on the caliper.

removing the nut from the rear shock to fully remove the belt guard. Remove the belt from the pulley and slide the rear wheel out.

Remove the stock caliper by unbolting the two mounting bolts from the caliper to the bracket. Lift the caliper up out of the way but do not remove the brake line yet, we'll do that when we're ready to hook up the new caliper.

Take the stock caliper bracket off the swingarm and install the new PM caliper bracket. The bracket should line up with the axle hole, and the bracket should stay snug on the swingarm. You'll be replacing the stock axle spacer with the new left-side spacer supplied in the PM caliper kit.

Slide the rear belt back onto the pulley, lift the rear wheel, and install the rear axle with the new spacer between the PM bracket and swingarm. Tighten the axle to the torque spec listed in your service manual and reinstall the belt guard and shock bolt.

Next you'll place the caliper over the rotor and align the mounting holes to the bracket. This is where the project requires some patience and direct attention. We need to center the caliper over the brake rotor. The center of the caliper is where the two halves of the caliper are joined together.

You'll need to look down from the top of the caliper to the rotor. If the caliper has an offset to the outside, then you'll need to use the caliper shim kit supplied with the caliper. The shims are mounted between the caliper and the caliper's mounting bracket. This will center the caliper over the rotor's center line. Install the shims by sliding the shim into place and replacing the mounting bolt.

Once you've centered the caliper, remove the bolts again and give them some blue Loctite. Then reinstall from the wheel side of the caliper and torque the bolts to 22 ft-lbs. Turn the wheel slowly to check for caliper-to-rotor interference.

Attach the brake line to the caliper with the banjo bolt. To bleed the brake system, it's best to have an extra set of hands to do the pumping of the pedal while you work the bleeder screw. Fill the master cylinder to the correct fill level if any fluid was lost. Attach a short length of rubber hose to the bleeder screw on the caliper and place the other end in a catch can. Push down and pump the pedal a few times and hold it down, open the bleeder fitting on the caliper with ¼-inch line wrench. You should have air and brake fluid coming out the end of the hose connected to the bleeder screw.

When the fluid and air stop coming out, close the bleeder screw and release the pedal. Repeat this several times because bleeding brakes can take a few passes. Air can "hide" in those lines. Don't be surprised if after a few miles you need to bleed the system again.

During the installation process, be sure to maintain proper brake fluid level in the master cylinder because too low a level will cause more air to get in the line. Never over-tighten the bleeder screw, and be sure to bleed all the air from the brake line. Failing to do so could result in poor performance of the brakes.

Spin the wheel and apply the brake pedal to ensure proper wheel stopping. Once it all checks out, allow about a 100-mile break-in period. Test the brakes at short riding intervals at slow speeds. Try to avoid unnecessary hard braking and inspect the disc and pads after your test rides for any uneven wear, warping, or loose fittings.

You can apply this procedure to the front or rear caliper changes for most models. Be sure to refer to your service manual for torque specs and always read the instructions supplied with the kit before tackling any task.

Wheel change, tire change

Since we're down low on the bike, let's talk wheels and tires. You only have two pieces of rubber between you and the road. That sentence alone should be enough to make you realize the importance of tire and wheel inspections. On a daily basis I see a bike with bad tires. I can't believe people actually get on their bikes and go for a ride without looking at their tires. The way your bike handles is directly related to the way you care for your wheels and tires. You should always check them for damage and wear.

This next task will take about seven seconds to do and it's one of the most important steps in maintaining your bike: Checking your air pressure.

The amount of air your tires should hold is listed on the motorcycle frame on newer models and is listed in your manual. I check the air pressure at least once a week if I'm not riding very often, and always before each ride. If it's been a few weeks and I haven't been able to get out on my bike for a ride, I will move my bike so the tires don't develop a soft spot from resting too long in one place.

Checking your tires and air pressure is an important way we read what the bike is telling us. Look at the tread for uneven wear or dry rot cracks. If you see anything like this you will want to replace those tires. And don't be cheap when it comes to tires. Again, you only have two pieces of rubber between you and the road. If you stumble across a nail head sticking out of your tire, don't leave it in and ride, change the tire. Uneven wear on the tread of your tires could be telling you a wheel bearing is bad or something in your front end could be off balance.

I often have customers come in the shop and ask me to check the wheel bearings on their bike because it's handling funny. Nine times out of ten when I check the air pressure I discover how low the tires are on air. Proper air pressure is directly related to how your bike is going to handle and prematurely wearing out your tires. If you want to stay safe and keep your bike running smooth, check your air pressure every time you get on your bike.

If you ride every day, you're probably thinking, "Do I really need to check my air pressure every time I ride?" Well, I look at it this way: What if on the way home last night you picked up a nail and overnight you slowly lost air, not enough to visibly see but enough to make your bike handle differently? Isn't it easier to deal with the few moments it took to check the pressure versus being out on the road on a bike that is handling poorly? It takes seven seconds people, come on! This is your bike and your body, take care of them.

You should also be looking at your axle nuts to make sure they are tight. Your wheels are important to look at also. If you have mag wheels, look them over for any dents. If you have a bike lift, you can lift the bike and run a straight edge along the wheel to feel for any low or high spots. Sometimes these can be invisible. You should see a difference when you freely spin the wheel if the bike is lifted.

If you have spoke wheels, or are thinking of getting some, see Project 16 for information on keeping them nice and tight.

PROJECT 14	Changing Tires

Tools Needed: Socket for axle, pliers, torque wrench

Time: 45 minutes to an hour per wheel   **Talent:** Intermediate

Cost: Average price for tires, $130–$180 (depending on brand and style, i.e., whitewalls, blackwalls)

Parts required: Tire, inner tube, and rim strip (for tube-type wheels), cotter pin

Performance Gain: A good piece of rubber between you and the road.

SERVICE INTERVALS

This is a ridiculous case of tire neglect. This tire needed changing many, many miles ago! Never let your treads wear down this low.

Tire care

Anytime you have the tires or inner tubes replaced, make sure the wheel is then properly balanced. Strange wear on the tire could be related to the way the wheel was balanced, as well as worn wheel bearings or steering head bearings. Your bike is always feeding you information from these inspections and services you perform.

If you want to save money when it's time for new tires, you can take the wheels off yourself and bring them in to the shop to have tires mounted to the wheel and then balanced. You can also change the tire yourself with some tire spoons, but trust me, with plenty of years of experience changing tires by hand, it's not worth it.

Chances are you probably don't have a wheel balancer, and your wheels will need balancing when a new tire is installed. There are two ways you can balance a wheel: gravity and dynamic. Wheels need balance to rotate smoothly to balance out the heavy and light areas. When properly

102

Any covers, like this axle cover, will obviously need to be removed first for access and wheel removal.

The caliper will need to be removed when taking the wheel off for a tire change.

For this style of front end, an Allen socket and ratchet are needed for axle removal.

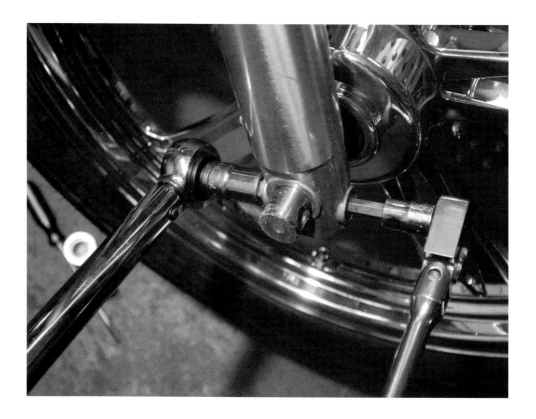

You can find the tire size printed on the sidewall and listed in your service manual. You'll need this information when it's time to replace your tread, so you should keep it handy.

balanced, weight is added to the light areas to "balance" out the wheel.

A bubble balancer uses gravity to indicate the balance, a lot like a level used for carpentry. Dynamic balancers, also known as spin balancers, spin the wheel at about 40 mph and use a reading to determine the balance. A spin balancer is rather expensive and is not practical for the home-based shop. A bubble gravity balancer is not as expensive, but for

maintaining your own bike this is not a necessary purchase. I recommend taking the wheel down to your local shop to have it balanced.

Let's talk a little about rubber. What brand tire should you use? What compound: radial or bias-ply? I have this conversation daily at my shop with customers. A bias-ply tire is constructed of layers of rubber-coated plies consisting of textile cords, usually nylon. The plies are

Make sure to note the tire air-pressure levels printed on the frame decal or in your service manual. The tire will have its maximum air pressure level imprinted on the sidewall. Tire pressure should be checked cold before the bike is ridden.

When replacing the tire, you will need to pay attention to the rotational direction of the tire in relation to the wheel. Generally, an arrow is molded into the tire sidewall. Not all tires are directional; some can be mounted either way.

placed upon each other at about 30-degree angles. These plies are then wrapped around the bead wires which hold the tire to the rim to create the casing or "air chamber." The plies then get covered with more rubber to create the tread pattern.

A radial tire is made up in two parts. A single layer of rubber-coated steel cables arch from one bead to the other to form the tire casing. Next, numerous rubber-coated steel belts are placed in the crown under the tread to form a strong stabilizing unit.

Bias-ply tires are most commonly used for motorcycles but radial tires are just as popular. Whichever you choose, never mix a radial with a bias-ply on the same bike. Keep the tires the same, front and back. It's also not recommended to have different tread patterns from front to back. Stay with the same tire on both your front and back wheels.

A tire machine makes installing a tire quicker and much safer, especially on new wheels. Tire spoons can slip and damage the rim—not a good idea after a large investment in new wheels.

TIRE MARKINGS

Note: Tire markings on chart are representational, and actual tire markings may differ from shown.

1	Brand name and registered trademark.
2	Type of tread pattern.
3	Name of product line.
4	Nominal section width, expressed in mm
5	Ratio between tire section height and nominal section width. This ratio is not indicated when section width is expressed in inches (eg. 3.50-18).
6	Code for tire construction: ("-": Bias, "R": Radial, "B", Bias Belted).
7	Nominal rim diameter size in inches
8	"Motorcycle" in abbreviated form. Differentiates motorcycle tires and rims from those designed for other vehicles. Shown on some models only.
9	Speed symbol. Indicates the tire's speed.
10	Tubeless (TL)
11	Expresses the tire's maximum load capacity (pounds) at the pressure indicated (psi)
12	Indicates where the tire was produced.
13	Abbreviation of "Department of Transportation". Serves to indicate that the tire conforms to the regulations issued by the Transport Dept's of USA and Canada.
14	The arrows indicate the direction of rotation of the tire according to the fitting position (front-rear).
15	For tires suitable for speeds over 130 mph / 210 km. Number indicates load index, e.g. 58 = 520lb. / 236kg
16	Number of plies and material.
17	Tread Wear Indicator.
18	DOT (Stands for Dept. of Transportation) This is the serial # for the tire, and the last 3 or 4 numbers represent the date. Example 3801 means the tire was produced in the 38th week of 2001.
19	Load and Speed Index codes

SAFETY WARNING!

While every effort has been taken with the production of this brochure and the information herein, Metzeler accepts no liability for loss or damage resulting from errors or omissions.

Remember what I said: You only have two pieces of rubber between you and the road.

How about tire sizes? Everyone these days wants to throw some fat rubber on the back. However, you really should stick with the stock tire size. Using a wider tire on a stock rim can be dangerous. If you want a fat tire, then get yourself set up with a chassis and wheel designed for a fat tire. Of course, there are fat tire kits you can use on your stock bike such as Performance Machine's Phat-Tail kit. These kits come with the correct parts needed to install a wider tire on your chassis correctly without jeopardizing function. Be sure to check their website for technical information on the kit.

The sizes printed on your tire represent the width, aspect, load rating, and speed rating. Let's take the very common Harley-Davidson rear application, the Dunlop

D401 130/90/B16 73H. The 401 represents the manufacturer's designation of tread style and model. The 130 is the width of the tire in millimeters. The 90 represents the aspect ratio or height. This means the tire is 90 percent as tall as it is wide. The B stands for it being a belted tire. The number 16 is the rim diameter in inches, the 73 is the load capacity, and H is the speed rating (see chart).

In order to figure out what tire you should use, you need to know what it is you want to get out of the tire. Like most things in life you can't have your cake and eat it to. What is your riding style and what type of bike are you riding? These are the questions you start with. You need to determine if you would be better off with a stickier compound and a softer tire for tearing it up and grabbing the turns, or with a harder compound suited better for higher miles and a heavier load. If you're riding a Sportster and are throwing

When mounting a new tire on the wheel, tire lube is used to make the tire more pliable.

Even with a tire machine, care should be taken not to damage the rim.

the bike around in the turns, then I'm going to recommend a softer compound to grab the road better. If you ride a dresser that's packed to the gills for long road trips, then a harder compound would be best for you.

Now that we have an idea of what compound to use, what brand should we choose? Dunlop, Metzler, Avon, Michelin, Continental? Honestly, you really need to try them all and "feel" what suits you best. I personally have tried many brands on my bike. I started with the stock Dunlop, and then I tried the Michelin Commander. Just as I found the Metzler Comp tire, which I really liked, they took it out of their lineup. Now I'm trying the Metzler ME880. Talk with the salesperson to help you decide what tire you should try.

Once the new tire is mounted, it is filled with air to the correct air pressure amount listed in the service manual.

When tires are made at the manufacturing plant, a release agent is used in the mold so the tire won't stick to it. That release agent stays on the tire and can make for a slick ride at first. When you have new tires installed on your bike, be cautious for the first 50 miles or so until the tire scuffs in and that release agent is worn off.

To remove the front wheel, you'll need to have the bike lifted properly and securely. Remove the caliper mounting hardware and let the caliper hang loose. Once the caliper is off the rotor, don't grab the lever or you'll force the caliper piston out and the caliper will need to be taken completely apart to re-seat it.

ACCESSORY HASSLES

Some people accessorize their bikes with all kinds of flashy covers and gadgets. Sure, these can look nice and add some flair to your bike but they tend to make service work more of a hassle. Axle nut covers are just two more bolts to contend with during wheel removal. The worst are brake rotor and caliper covers. I don't want to hurt anyone's feelings if they have these on their bike, but they are a major pain! The tiny bolts that are used to hold them on are very easily stripped and we all know what a stripped bolt can do to your day. I'm also not a big advocate of rotor covers because they don't allow as much air on the rotor. Excessive heat can warp a rotor, which will affect the braking on your bike. Your rotors should be getting as much air as they can. Big "flying saucer" disc covers will retain the heat from the friction of the brake pads.

Go ahead and remove the axle nut depending on the front end you have. This will be different for certain models. Refer to your service manual for axle removal. When sliding the axle out, be sure to pay attention to spacer position. Wheel spacers are going to fall off when the axle is pulled out so you must pay attention to their exact location. I usually lay them down on the side of the bike they came off and the order in which they came off. You can now take your front wheel in for a new tire.

The rear wheel is very similar. Go ahead and remove the rear caliper from the wheel and get it out of the way. Remove your axle nut and pull the axle out, remembering to pay attention to rear wheel spacers. You'll need to make sure the belt or chain is off the pulley or sprocket.

When replacing the wheels, make sure you replaced the spacers the same way and re-torque the axle nuts according to the specs in your service manual. Replace the calipers to their caliper-mounting bracket and test the brakes by spinning the wheel and applying pressure to the lever and pedal. Replace any cotter pins that you removed with new ones. You can pick those up at any bike shop or hardware store.

Most important, don't forget that the new tread will be slick for the first few miles. Not too much throttle and not too much brake until it wears in.

One way to balance a wheel is with a gravity balancer pictured here. Every time a tire or inner tube is changed on your wheel, it will need to be balanced.

PROJECT 15	Wheel Upgrade (Performance Machine)

Tools Needed: Ratchet and socket to remove axle, pliers, Allen or torx socket, torque wrench, dial indicator for checking bearing play

Time: Average 90 minutes per wheel   **Talent:** Experienced

Cost: Polished: $800 per wheel. Chrome-plated: $1,000. Other parts: $35.

Parts required: (most supplied with new wheel) Wheels, bearings, wheel seals, grease, axle spacers

Performance Gain: This is mainly an aesthetic improvement. Aftermarket wheels can give your bike a personal touch, they're easy to clean, and they are often lighter than stock wheels—and every reduction in weight contributes to handling and speed.

Stock wheels on motorcycles are, for the most part, fine. That is, if you like the wheels the bike came with, usually mag or wire wheels. One downfall to stock wheels is trying to keep them clean. The cast metal wheels are very susceptible to becoming pitted and are nearly impossible to keep clean. Stock wire wheels come equipped with zinc untreated spokes that just look awful no matter how much effort you put into cleaning them.

Wheels have a major impact on how the bike handles as well as how it looks. Adding a set of custom wheels will make your bike look so much better, not to mention aid in the maintenance of wheel care. And if you are performance minded, billet wheels will lighten the load of your sled.

Picking a set of custom wheels isn't easy. Which do you use, billet or cast? Most aftermarket wheel manufacturers use 6061 T6 aluminum. The 6061 represents this alloy as

You get the best of both worlds, looks and performance, when upgrading to a good set of wheels.

110

To set the bearings in the new PM wheels, we bolted the old caliper to the wheel and set our dial indicator to measure bearing end play.

A bearing packer tool makes packing the bearings with grease cleaner and saves time.

If you don't have a bearing packer tool, the old method of hand packing works fine—just a little messier. Place a pile of grease in the palm of your hand and push the grease into the bearing until you see it come through the rollers.

Here the new wheel bearings and seals are all packed with fresh new grease.

Above left: The inner wheel spacer will also need to be greased before being placed inside the wheel. Above right: Here is a freshly packed wheel bearing placed in the wheel.

forged aluminum, which is very durable. T6 is the heat-treating of the metal. Billet wheels are more expensive than cast, but, like anything in the motorcycle world, you get what you pay for. The reason billet wheels are normally priced higher is the cost of high-grade aluminum and the amount of machine time spent on each wheel. When deciding what wheel to use, keep in mind the strength-to-weight ratio is better with billet than with 6061 aluminum. This means a billet wheel is going to be lighter and stronger.

For this project, I decided to upgrade the stock mag wheels to a set of polished Performance Machine (PM) wheels on a 1996 XL. Performance Machine has been manufacturing wheels since 1975; we're talking top-of-the-line here. Since we are removing the wheels from the bike, and the tires were showing some wear, we decided to go ahead and add some new rubber.

First we need to set the bearings in the new wheels. Performance Machine wheels are shipped with all the hardware

With the wheel bearing in place, the greased wheel seal is last to get set in the new wheel.

needed for the job. To check the endplay, have the inner bearing spacer in the wheel hub, place each bearing (ungreased) in their race, but do not install the wheel seals at this time. Use the axle, with a piece of pipe or tubing to take up the gap, and torque down to the listed axle torque spec. Measure the endplay with a dial indicator. If you have a magnetic indicator, you can mount the rotor to the wheel and set the indicator on the rotor. You lengthen or shorten the endplay by adjusting the inner bearing spacer. Example: If the endplay is fifteen-thousandths of an inch and you need six-thousandths, you'll need to remove nine thousandths from the spacer by filing or machining it down. If you don't have enough endplay, add shims to the spacer. They're available in different thicknesses.

The new bearings will need to be packed with fresh grease once the proper endplay has been set. A bearing grease tool comes in handy for this messy job. If you don't have one, the old method of hand packing works just as well. Place a slab of grease on the palm of your hand and work the bearing into the pile until you see the grease oozing out from the opposite side between the rollers.

A large socket works well for pressing the wheel seal into the wheel evenly.

Once the bearings have been set properly, it's time to throw some rubber on the wheel. Take your time to protect the investment you just made.

Next we will mount the new tires on the PM wheels. You can take these wheels to a shop to have the tires mounted and balanced, which I recommend. You can still install tires by hand with tire spoons, but with brand-new wheels you'll want to be real careful not to slip with the tire spoon and gouge the rim.

Once the tire is on the wheel, it will next need to be balanced. Each manufacturer will use a different balance marking. Again, this is often a job that's easier to leave up to your local shop.

If you are using your stock rotors and pulley, you'll need to remove those from your stock wheels and place them on the new wheels. It's recommended you use new rotor and pulley hardware. A nice finishing touch to the look of a new set of wheels is to match the rotors and pulley to the design of the wheel. We opted for that on this bike and,

honestly, I think it's the only way to go. If you're going to do it, do it right!

The new tires are mounted and balanced on the Performance Machine wheels, we have added the PM matching rotors and pulley, and now we're ready to install them on the bike. Lift the bike properly and secure it down. Remove the caliper from the bracket and let it hang loose and out of your way. If you are performing a caliper upgrade, now is a good time since the caliper and wheel are off the bike. Remove the rear wheel and note the axle adjuster settings at this time. It will be a good starting point to adjust the belt or chain when re-installing.

Install the new wheel carefully, be gentle, and take your time. You just made a large investment and working slowly and carefully is an insurance policy to keep those wheels

Before removing the rear wheel, note your belt adjustment on the axle adjuster with a marker. This will be a good starting point when readjusting the belt tension.

If any sheet metal is in the way, you'll want to remove it to ensure it doesn't get damaged.

Remove the old wheels once the bike is lifted and secured properly. Slide the belt off the pulley, or the chain from the sprocket.

When installing the new rotors and pulley on the wheels, be sure to use new hardware and blue Loctite on the bolts.

If you removed any other bolts, as we did here with this shock mount bolt, be sure to tighten them back to torque specs.

Tighten the axle last, and be sure to torque to the specs listed in the service manual.

looking mint. Reinstall the wheel using the stock outer spacers, unless the new wheel is supplied with its own spacers. At this time, adjust the rear chain or belt.

On the front end, the tire might not fit past the fender bolts so it will be necessary to remove the fender.

Once you have the wheel installed, mount the brake caliper back onto the bracket. Tighten the axle back up to the torque spec listed in your manual and reinstall the axle cotter pin. Always spin the wheel and inspect the brakes to ensure that they're working properly.

Always use a new cotter pin on the axle every time you remove it.

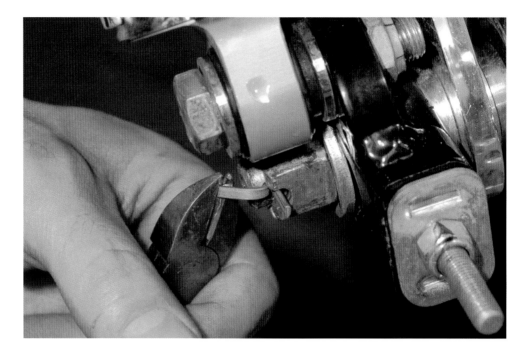

Matching the rotors and pulley to the new Performance Machine wheel design, as shown here, obviously adds the finishing touches.

PROJECT 16 | Wire Wheel Care

Tools Needed: Spoke wrench, a shop with a truing stand

Time: Average, one hour per wheel

Talent: Intermediate

Cost: A few bucks for a spoke wrench, but mostly time

Parts required: Unless you find a spoke that needs replacing, no parts are required for this job.

Performance Gain: It's part of maintaining your wheels properly for optimal performance and longevity.

It amazes me how many bikes come in for a tire change and we'll find loose spokes. Usually the customer has no idea he or she should be looking at the spokes for tightness. One time I had a customer come in for a tire before taking a 600-mile trip. When we got the wheel off we found five broken spokes! We made sure he was taken care of with new spokes before his trip. His departure was delayed, but it sure was better leaving late than not getting there at all.

Like everything else on your bike, inspecting your tires and wheels is going to tell you a story about your bike. If you have spoked wheels, check each spoke for tightness. Any loose spokes will need to be tightened with a spoke wrench. If you find the spokes to be a little loose, you'll need to tighten them in a set pattern to not throw the wheel out of true.

"True" means to have the wheel run straight side to side and up and down. Loose or broken spokes will cause your

A truing stand should be used to check the true of the wheel. Most home-based workshops won't have a truing stand, so bring your wire wheel to a shop to have this checked.

wheel to warp and change shape over time. Obviously, this is a huge problem when a major wheel malfunction occurs on the road.

You'll start with the spoke closest to the valve stem. Using a spoke torque wrench, give it a quarter-turn or to the designated torque on the wheel. Skip the next two spokes and tighten the next spoke the same way. Make your way around the wheel tightening every fourth spoke. At the starting point, start over moving forward one spoke. Continue all the way around until all spokes have been tightened. Never tighten a spoke more than a quarter turn at a time.

If you perform these inspections regularly, you should be on top of the game and only need a routine tightening here or there.

If a wheel is really out of whack (i.e., missing or broken spokes), the wheel is going to need to be trued after spoke repair. The correct way to true a wheel is to have the wheel off the bike and placed on a truing stand. Again, this is not a practical tool for you to have in your shop so the best bet would be to bring the wheel in to a mechanic.

Inspecting your wheels on a regular basis should prevent you from a disaster like the five broken spokes my customer had.

You'll need a spoke wrench if you find a loose spoke during wire wheel inspections. A certain pattern must be followed when tightening the spokes on wire wheels.

PROJECT 17	Final Chain and Belt Adjustment

Tools Needed: Socket for axle nut, belt adjustment tool, pliers, torque wrench

Time: 15 minutes   **Talent:** Beginner   **Cost:** None   **Parts required:** None

Performance Gain: If your final drive chain or belt is worn or out of adjustment, it can really affect the power delivered to your rear wheel, not to mention causing failure on the road. Make this part of your regular inspection.

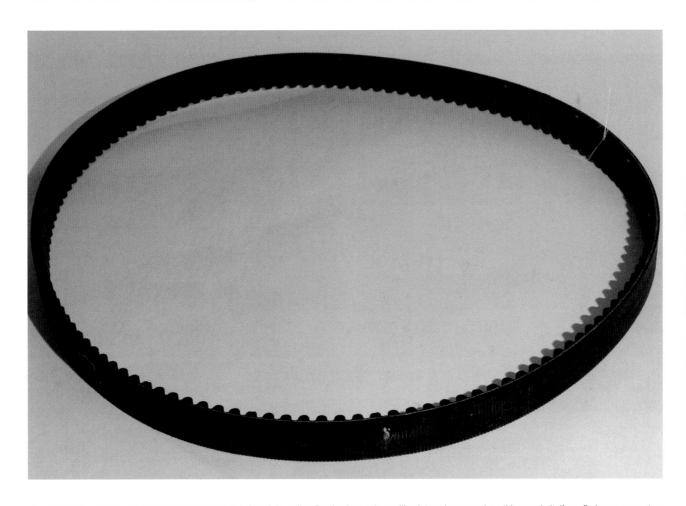

You can clearly see that a rock is lodged between this belt and the pulley. Routine inspections will point out issues such as this worn belt. If you find any wear or tear in your final belt, you will need to replace it.

The final drive belt or chain on your bike is also going to need inspection on a regular basis. You'll be looking for any wear, cracking, loss of teeth, or any rocks that got imbedded in the belt. Look at the sprocket or pulley while inspecting the belt or chain. If you see any chips, gouges, tooth damage, or chrome chips that could damage the belt, you'll want to have that pulley or sprocket replaced. This is when having a bike lift comes in handy so you can freely spin the rear wheel when lifted to see how the final belt or chain moves.

The specs for tension on the chains and belts are of course listed in your manual. You should be checking belt

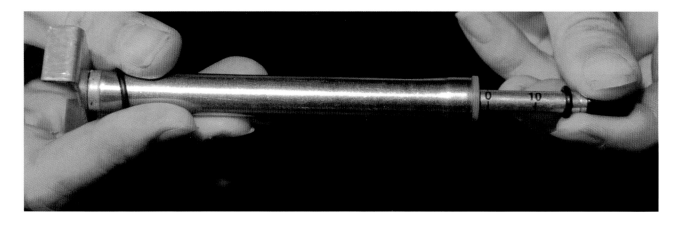

A belt tension gauge, another motorcycle specialty tool, is used to measure the free play of the final drive belt.

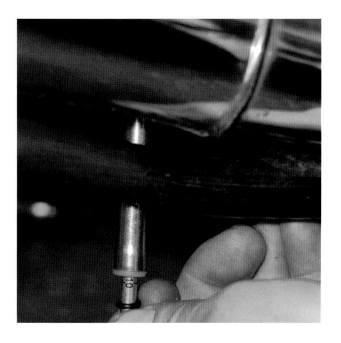

Place the belt tension tool on the lower side of the belt, take a measurement, push the tool up so it reads 10 pounds of force, and check how far the belt moved. Compare this to the listed play measurement in your manual.

To make a belt adjustment, loosen the locknut, turn the adjusting bolt to adjust the tension, and repeat the same for the opposite side.

tension with your bike cold. Place the bike in neutral and apply 10 pounds of upward force on the lower part of the belt or chain. Rotate the belt to find the tightest spot. For example, on Sportsters, the belt movement should be no more than ¾₆ to ¹¹⁄₁₆ of an inch. (Check your service manual for your model's tension.)

If adjustment is needed, remove the cotter pin on the axle and loosen the axle nut. Turn the axle adjuster nuts on each side of the bike clockwise to decrease tension and counterclockwise to increase. Be sure to turn each adjuster the same number of turns to maintain wheel alignment.

Once the proper adjustment is achieved, tighten the axle nut to the listed torque spec and reinstall the cotter pin in the axle.

If you're adding a master link to a chain you must be sure the clip is going the proper way. I see this placed backwards on so many bikes and it's so dangerous.

Standard chains will need to be maintained and lubricated routinely. O-ring chains are self-lubricating.

Any time you gear up for a ride you should be performing this quick inspection on your bike along with everything else. All it takes is a few seconds to make sure everything checks out. Then you'll feel that much more comfortable and confident on your ride.

PROJECT 18	S&S Serious Bang for the Buck Quick Setup Kit

Tools Needed: Screwdriver, sockets to fit muffler bolts, ¼-inch Allen, ¾-inch open-end wrench, Phillips screwdriver, torx bit

Time: 90 minutes   **Talent:** Intermediate   **Cost:** About $500

Parts required: Blue Loctite, carb-to-manifold seal

Performance Gain: Big horsepower for the buck

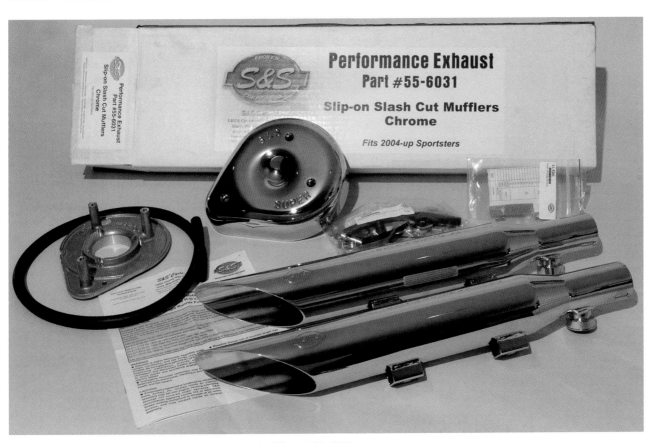

You'll get everything you need to increase you horspower with this all-in-one kit by S&S.

Since you're taking on the responsibility of maintaining your bike, it won't be long before you're ready to bump up the horsepower on your ride. Wanting your bike to run faster and better happens in a short time. Sooner or later it will happen to you, and you'll find yourself wishing for more throttle.

S&S Cycle sells a quick setup kit that will produce a big horsepower increase for little money. Ten horses for $500 is a good deal. The movie *Mad Max* had this little mechanic hop-up shop with a sign in the window that read, "How fast do you want to go? How much money do you have?" That says it all, horsepower costs money.

The great feature of this quick setup kit by S&S is that you can install this kit yourself. The kit consists of slip-on mufflers, jets for your stock CV carb, a new air filter, and a new air cleaner. If your bike is still in stock condition, this setup was designed for you. You're getting everything that you could possibly want to change on your bike all at once.

We ran this XL on the dyno in its stock condition. The horsepower in this stock bike was 60.

To start the S&S upgrade project, remove the stock air filter and housing and replace them with the new S&S parts.

The factory air cleaner backing plate's small inlet restricts air flow.

Above: Remove the carb top cover to access the needle in the slider. Above right, below left and below right: Remove the old needle and replace it with the S&S-supplied needle. Reinstall the retainer once the new needle is in place.

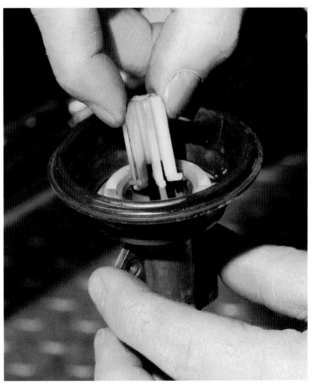

Replace the slide assembly into the carb body (it only fits one way), then the spring, followed by the carb top.

Remove the float bowl, and have a catch pan ready for any fuel.

I picked this 2004 Sportster since other than the 1200 upgrade (cylinders and pistons) and some cosmetic accessories, everything is stock. We decided to show you the results of this S&S kit with a dyno printout so you could see the actual horsepower gain. Once the funds build back up, the next step for this bike will be a brake system upgrade to compensate for the engine mods.

We ran the bike as-is on the dyno and you can see from the charts this bike was lacking a little at only 60 horsepower. The next step was to dig in and install the kit.

You'll start off first by removing the air cleaner and filter. We'll remove the carb to change the stock jets with the new jets equipped in the kit. The S&S kit comes with a small diagram of a base jetting to work with; this is a good starting point. (Note: You may need to change the jetting again so don't put all those tools away.) We loosened the idle mixture screw for finer tuning of the idle and installed a 45 low-speed pilot jet and a 180 main jet. You'll also replace the needle with the one supplied in the kit. We'll see how it goes after our second dyno run to find out if another jet change will be necessary.

Follow the instructions in your service manual for changing jets. Replace the carb back on the bike and use a new carb-to-manifold seal.

To install the new air filter and air cleaner, assemble both head breather bolt assemblies according to the drawing

Above, above right and below right: Using a small flathead screwdriver, remove the main jet from the emulsion tube and replace it with the suggested starting jet from the S&S kit. Also, replace the pilot jet which is recessed into the carb body next to the main jet, and replace the float bowl.

equipped with the S&S kit. Next, screw the breather assemblies into breather vent holes in the heads. Don't over-tighten at this time. Install a rubber T-hose over the cylinder head breather fittings with the hose "T" toward the rear of the engine. The hose will need to be trimmed to the needed length. Make sure it's not twisted or kinked. Once the hose is fitted, secure the T-hose to the breather fittings with black zip ties or metal clamps provided with the kit.

Now you can tighten the head breather vent bolts using red Loctite. Insert the 1/4-28 bolt through the backing plate from the filter side. On Big Twins this will need the ⅛ inch thick spacer between the back plate and support bracket. (This is mapped out in the S&S instructions, please refer to them for your specific model of bike.)

The next step is to install the bracket, flat washer, and nyloc nut. Repeat this step for the other mounting bracket.

Go ahead and align the back plate on the carburetor but do not over-tighten at this time. The screws supplied for the back plate by S&S come ready to go with locking compound on them. However, if you are using different screws than the ones supplied with the kit, be sure to use blue Loctite.

Next, align the mounting brackets with the head breather bolts and secure with the back plate screw. Don't over-tighten at this time. To position the mounting brackets on carbureted models, align the backing plate and

brackets and then tighten all the mounting hardware. If you have a fuel-injected model, reference the instructions provided for mounting the brackets. Use a zip tie or metal clamp over the "T" of the hose, insert the half-inch steel tube part way into the "T," and tighten the clamp. Slide the short length of beveled hose over the half-inch steel tube with the beveled end out and facing down. Tighten the clamp. Use a drop of blue Loctite on the threads and install nuts and lock washers. Now tighten all hardware. Torque specs are listed in the instructions.

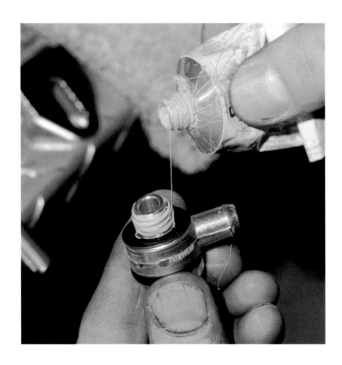

Use sealer or thread-locker on the new supplied breather bolts, and follow instructions using the breather hose to align the fittings and tighten the bolts.

Attach the hose extension and metal tube to the breather hose setup.

Use a drop of blue Loctite on the bracket bolts and snug them into the breather bolts. Don't tighten them until everything is lined up.

Install the new filter element and the air cleaner cover with the supplied hardware.

Now we'll replace the stock mufflers with the performance mufflers in the S&S kit. Remove the muffler bolts and gently pull the stock mufflers off the bike. Replace with the performance mufflers and tighten bolts using blue Loctite. Refer to your service manual for torque specs.

Once we had all these parts installed, we ran the bike again on the dyno. You can clearly see the horsepower difference between the run before and after the S&S kit install. We had a significant horsepower gain of eight, which is clearly felt out on the road. Like the sign said in *Mad Max*, horsepower equals money and this kit is worth every penny—and it's a breeze! Easy to install, high quality, and good value—a rare find!

Tighten the mounting bolts to the backing plate once everything is aligned.

Use either the supplied clamp or a zip tie to attach the breather hose to the fitting.

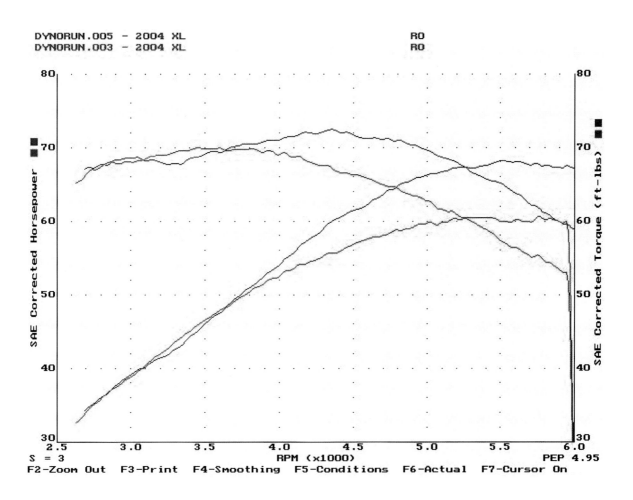

Install the S&S-supplied air filter and tighten the new classic S&S air cleaner cover.

Remove the muffler mounting bolts and clamp, and gently pull the stock muffler off. You may have to loosen the pipe at the cylinder head to get the muffler off the crossover tube. Above right and opposite top left: Remove the gasket from the stock muffler and reinstall it in the S&S muffler.

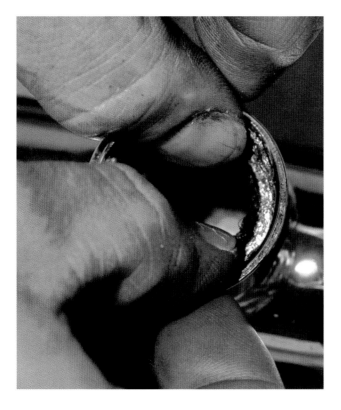

Slide the clamp onto the new muffler and install the muffler to the head pipe.

Once the kit was installed, we made our second run on the dyno and found the bike's power had increased by eight horses! Not bad for a couple of hours.

PROJECT 19	Cleaning your Bike

Tools Needed: Spray-on cleaner, drying towels, detailer, metal polish

Time: 30 minutes

Talent: Beginner

Cost: A few dollars for supplies, but remember the old saying "You get what you pay for." There are a lot of cheap cleaning products out there.

Parts required: None

Performance Gain: Your only gain here is beauty. But washing your bike is a great opportunity to inspect and locate any problems.

OK, you're probably sick of this saying, but one more time: Your bike is an extension of your body. You need to treat your bike the same way you treat your body. With that said, I'm hoping you bathe yourself regularly, because if some people treat their bodies the same as their bike, then there are some stinky, dirty people walking around out there.

Why is it important to clean your bike? Well, for one, your bike will look nice and it will help your resale value. But more important, when cleaning your bike you will be forced to look at it and see any problems that need to be addressed. It still amazes me to see a bike come in my shop totally filthy, and when I clean that bike I'll find some missing bolts or cracks in the frame or another important issue.

Using a metal polish on your bike will get you up close and force you to look at areas you might otherwise not pay attention to.

A spray-on bike wash, such as Wizard's Power Clean, will make cleaning fast and easy. Just spray it on and hose it off!

R.T., my boyfriend and business partner, once found a crack in his Springer front end when cleaning his old iron-head chopper. There's no better way to inspect your bike than to clean it; you're killing two birds with one stone.

I like to start cleaning with a spray-on cleaner like Wizard's Power Clean. A spray-on cleaner is so much easier to work with than the old conventional bucket-and-sponge method. The cleaning job will get done much faster with a spray-on cleaner. Make sure you use an acid-free cleaner that is safe to use on aluminum and paint. Spray the cleaner on and hose it off. Nothing to it.

Once you get the bike washed off, it's time for detailing. This is your chance to really get up-close with your bike and look at everything. Rubbing polish on parts and buffing them clean will get you looking at parts on your bike that you might not pay attention to at any other time.

If you just ride your bike and put it away dirty, you're leaving all that road debris behind to wear away at your metals and bolts. Corrosion will weaken things like oil and brake lines, fittings, calipers, rotors, bolts, nuts, etc. Look for exces-sive rust on bolts and replace them if they look bad. This is the perfect time to upgrade bolts to stainless steel. You'll never have to worry about rust again with stainless bolts.

Look for loose bolts, loose plug wires, worn belts, etc. If you find any loose bits and pieces, tighten or replace them.

If you come across any rust, you will want to clean that with a wire brush and remove all rust before painting the area to protect it. Look closely at what you're looking at; the rust could just be the result of a paint chip or it may be something worse, such as a crack in the part or a broken bolt.

Cleaning your bike is just one more chore on your list of tasks to properly maintain your bike.

CHAPTER 5
ELECTRICAL 101

BATTERIES

I put this topic off as long as I could, but we have to deal with it eventually, so let's get it out of the way. First, let me say if you plan to do any work to your bike other than basic inspections, you have to disconnect the battery cables so you don't accidentally start the bike. Always disconnect the negative cable first. The negative cable is grounded to the frame, so if you accidentally touch the frame or any other metal part, nothing bad will happen. If you disconnect the positive side first and accidentally touch the frame or other metal, you are creating a ground that will let the juice run right through you, maybe even start a fire.

To disconnect the negative cable on the battery, you'll need a 10-mm wrench. Make sure the cable won't be able to touch anything metal, like the frame. I usually stick a shop rag or a short piece of rubber hose around the terminal to be sure of no contact.

If you maintain your battery properly from the beginning, you should be able to get three to five years out of it. Let's talk about inspecting the battery. First, the battery contains a sulfuric acid solution as an electrolyte, and it can do some damage to your skin and eyes. One of my lucky jobs here at the shop is filling and charging batteries. I've had the acid spill on my clothes and have lost many a good pair of jeans to battery acid. Trust me, you don't want this stuff on you, so please wear eye protection and gloves when handling the battery. Most newer bikes come with a sealed battery, making it impossible for the acid to spill out, but you should always be cautious nonetheless.

When installing a new battery, it must be charged fully to ensure a long life. Follow the initial charging instructions that come with the new battery. The newer sealed-type batteries have different charging instructions than the earlier wet-cell types. If you fill your battery and only give it a quick charge because you're in too much of a hurry to ride,

These are prime examples of rusted and corroded battery terminals. Terminals in this condition can be the cause of hard starting problems.

If you will not be replacing the battery, use a piece of sandpaper or wire brush to clean corroded battery terminals.

This will almost always be the first step in any motorcycle servicing job—you'll need to remove the seat to gain access to the battery on almost every model.

Once the seat is removed, disconnect the battery cables to eliminate any chance of current still flowing. Always disconnect the negative first.

To charge the battery, it's best to have it off the bike. This is mostly a concern for acid-type batteries. Overcharging could cause the acid to overflow and do some serious damage to the bike.

A battery tender, like the one pictured, is best for charging your battery. Make sure the charger is not plugged in prior to connecting to the battery.

the second you hit the start button and put the battery under a load, you just guaranteed yourself a short battery life. If the battery wasn't charged correctly initially, it will never be able to fully charge. So, like anything in life, slow down, take your time, and do it right.

INSPECTING THE BATTERY AND CHARGING SYSTEM

The top of the battery should be clean from dirt and residue. If the cables and terminals have any oxidation or corrosion, you will need to clean them with a wire brush or a piece of sandpaper. Check all the fasteners for tightness and any breakage. Look at the battery posts to make sure they haven't been warped from overheating. Basically, look the whole battery over for cracks or warps.

If your bike won't start and it seems like the battery is dead, this is when a voltmeter is handy. Use the voltmeter to check the battery. More often than not you'll find that loose terminals, corrosion, frayed ends, or worn insulation leading to a short is more than likely the culprit of the dead battery. If you don't have a voltmeter, call your local shop to get your bike in for an appointment and have the shop do a voltage test for you.

A great, safe, and easy way to maintain the life of your battery is with a battery charger or tender. This will charge the battery for you and keep it fully charged, prolonging its life. When you hook the battery charger to the battery, red is for positive and black is for negative. A tender will tell you when the battery is fully charged.

If you're using a battery charger, I recommend you take the battery off the bike to charge it. If the battery would happen to overcharge, it can overflow and spill acid, doing things to your bike that won't be pretty. If you're using a motorcycle battery tender, you won't have to worry about overcharging. The battery tender will shut off automatically.

Make sure the tender or charger is turned off before you hook the battery up to it. Same thing when disconnecting.

Remember: Always disconnect the negative cable first when removing, and connect the negative cable last when reinstalling. If you do take the battery out of your bike to charge it, the positive gets disconnected last when removing, and connected first when reinstalling. Make sure you refer to your service manual before attempting battery removal.

PROJECT 20	Tech Cycle Starter Upgrade

Tools Needed: ³⁄₁₆-inch Allen socket, T27 torx bit, ¼-inch Allen socket with extension to reach starter bolts, pliers

Time: 1–2 hours

Talent: Intermediate

Cost: Approximately $600

Parts required: Primary gasket, primary fluid, primary inspection cover gasket, Tech Cycle starter kit

Performance Gain: You'll eliminate lagging when starting your bike, and get a starter with higher torque.

Believe it or not, there are a lot of parts available for your bike that perform better than stock. If a part on your bike fails and needs to be replaced, do a little research before you just replace it with a part equivalent to stock. You might be able to upgrade the part to a product that will perform better and be of higher quality. I've replaced a lot of starters on bikes, so I decided I'd walk you through a starter upgrade step-by-step.

First, I did my homework and found a manufacturer that had a solid product and reputation to boot. Tech Cycle Performance Products has been manufacturing high-performance starters for five years in the V-Twin industry. Tech Cycle builds their starters from the ground up, testing the sub-assemblies during the manufacturing process as well as the complete assembly prior to final cleaning and shipping.

You know you're getting a quality product with inspection like that from the manufacturer.

They have three starters to choose from. For this project, I decided to use the Tech 2.0kw (2.7-horsepower) Tornado starter. This starter is the number-one-rated starter on the market. This starter, and all Tech starters, feature a one-piece mounting plate/gearbox fully machined from 6061-T651 aircraft aluminum. If you have a high-compression engine, this starter can handle it. Remember: When making power increases, you'll need to compensate all other systems of your stock bike to compensate.

The first step to the starter upgrade project on this 1998 Softail is to have the service manual open to the starter section. You need to remove the seat to disconnect the battery so it can be removed from the bike. Take your drain pan

If your stock starter has some "lag" time, upgrade to a more performance-geared starter like this one from Tech Cycle.

Depending on the job, the primary cover may need to be removed. Be sure the fluid is drained prior to removal. To upgrade the starter you'll need access to the starter's jackshaft bolt inside the primary cover.

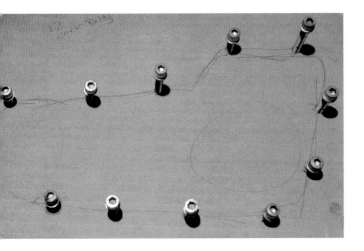

An easy way to remember the bolt pattern is to make a template of the primary cover on a piece of cardboard. The bolts will be kept in order and easy to locate when it's time to reinstall.

Above: The starter end cover on this Softail needed to be removed, along with a few other parts that were in the way, before I could remove the starter bolts. Top: Before removing the starter, the lock tab on the starter's jackshaft bolt inside the primary cover will need to be bent while holding the jackshaft drive gear. Middle: Often overlooked, the shaft nut will need to be removed before the starter can be taken off the bike.

Compare the stock starter (black, left) and the new high-performance Tech Cycle starter we are replacing it with. You can see the difference between the two.

and drain the primary fluid. You'll be using a ³⁄₁₆-inch Allen socket to remove the primary bolts. The inspection cover uses a T-27 torx bit.

When removing the primary bolts, it's a good habit to make a cardboard template of the primary bolt pattern so you'll know exactly where they came from when it's time to reinstall them.

Once the primary cover is off, unlock the starter shaft locktab. If you don't have a parts cleaner, and most people don't, you can clean the primary cover of old oil with a can of brake cleaner.

On the right side of the bike you'll need a long extension with a socket to remove the starter bolts. Of course, if there are any fancy covers in the way you'll need to remove them first. This is where those nice dress-up items become a bother. Once the bolts are out, go ahead and remove the starter. If anything is in the way, you'll need to make room. This bike is equipped with a Legends Air Ride kit, and we needed to move the compressor housing to make room for the starter to slip past.

Take the new starter and place some anti-seize on the jack shaft. Take your time installing the starter, making sure everything is lined up correctly. Tech starters come with a

Once all the starter bolts have been removed, carefully slide the old starter off the bike.

ELECTRICAL 101

A small amount of anti-seize should be placed on the starter jackshaft prior to reinstallation. This will prevent any galling on the moving surfaces.

Be careful when slipping the new starter into place on the chassis. Make sure the bolt holes line up and that the starter is in the correct position.

Don't forget to bend the lock tab on the starter jackshaft back into place before reinstalling the primary cover.

A parts cleaner is best for removing oily residue from parts. If you don't have a parts cleaner, set aside a utility tub specifically for solvent use. Here I am cleaning oil from the primary cover prior to reinstalling it.

heavy-duty battery cable that is "one size fits all." In order to get your proper cable measurement, simply put it on the bike, run it up to where it will connect to the battery, and mark the cable. Once you get your size, strip the rubber coating away so you can solder your connection. For this job we used a torch to solder the tab to the cable. Before soldering, place a piece of shrinkwrap below the connection. When the solder is complete, bring the shrinkwrap up over to cover the connection and heat it until it shrinks. A heat gun comes in handy for wiring.

Once everything is back in place, bolts have been tightened, and cables are in position, bend the starter shaft-lock tab. If you haven't already adjusted your primary chain, now is a great time since the cover is off and gives you plenty of room to work. Replace the primary cover, inspection cover, and drain plug, making sure to use thread sealant on the drain plug.

Always replace gaskets, never reuse them. Don't be cheap and try to reuse a gasket. You'll only be mad at yourself when you have to take the cover back off when the gasket leaks.

Fill your primary back to the service manual specs and tighten all bolts to torque specs. Reinstall the battery and you're ready to go. When I fired the bike, I could tell this was a successful job. Choosing the Tech Cycle starter was a great decision, the bike fired right away and sounded awesome. No more lagging or "tired sound" like the stock starter had.

The Tech starter came with a one-size-fits-all heavy-duty battery cable. I had to cut the length and strip the coating off in order to attach the terminal on the cable.

The terminal is crimped onto the battery cable with a set of wire crimpers.

Once you have the cable length cut and the coating removed from the cable, it's time to solder the terminal on the end of the battery cable.

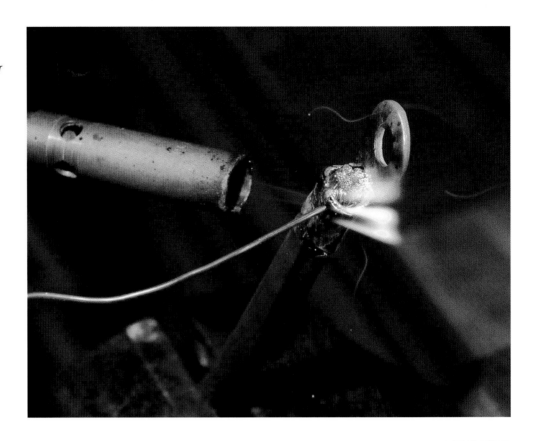

Like with any soldering connection, a piece of shrink tube is placed on the cable first so it can be moved up over the solder to insure a seal over the connection. A heat gun works best on shrink tube.

CHARGING SYSTEM

Basically there are two charging system setups on American V-Twin bikes. The early style consists of the battery, generator, and regulator. The generator creates a direct current (DC). The regulator maintains the voltage to the battery and all other units such as lights, ignition, etc., at a constant voltage unaffected by engine speed or load.

If for some reason you find yourself getting into the charging system on a generator-type bike and you disconnect the battery, the generator is going to have to be polarized before starting the engine. If you don't polarize the generator first, the charging system will work in the opposite manner and actually drain the battery voltage instead of maintaining or "regulating" it. One simple way to polarize the generator once the battery is reconnected is to take a piece of wire and touch the positive battery terminal and connect to the armature terminal of the generator. This is done before you start the bike.

Please refer to your service manual if you find yourself in need of charging system care and polarizing.

On later bikes, usually 1978 and up, the charging system consists of the battery, voltage regulator, and alternator (stator and rotor). The alternator is made up of the rotor, which is mounted on the engine sprocket shaft, and the stator bolted to the crankcase. The rotor, which contains magnets, spins along with the engine around the solidly mounted stator. The stator is a group of copper-wound coils. The rotor spinning around the stator creates an alternating current (AC) of approximately 30 to 50 volts. This current flows to a voltage rectifier/regulator. The regulator converts the AC current to the DC direct current that your battery requires. This unit also limits (regulates) the output it sends.

If the charging system on your bike is causing problems, the first place to start is at the battery. Again, you're checking those battery terminals and cables for corrosion and bad connections. If you see nothing visibly wrong, you'll want to inspect and test the charging system components. Refer to your service manual for all correct procedures if you want to perform the tasks yourself.

A very common problem with charging systems is the voltage regulator wire pulling out and away from the stator plug. Take two seconds to check that the voltage regulator plug is fully inserted in the stator plug (located on the forward side of your primary cover). It's the nature of the beast—vibration will shake things loose on a Harley. You can purchase voltage regulator retaining clips to keep that plug from backing out.

The ignition coil is responsible for sending the voltage from the regulator to the spark plug. The coil is basically a

The voltage regulator plug backing out of the stator plug is a very common charging problem, as you can see here. Always inspect this plug at the first sign of a charging problem.

Voltage regulator retaining clips like this one can be used to prevent the regulator plug backing out due to vibration.

transformer. It transforms the 12 volts from the battery into higher voltage to send to the spark plugs. Inside the coil there are two "coils" or windings, a primary and a secondary with a laminated iron core. This is all sealed in a watertight insulating compound. If tests show your coil is bad, it is not something you can rebuild or repair, you must replace it.

Your service manual will go into detailed explanations on how the ignition systems work on V-Twin engines. Please refer to that section of the service manual for more in-depth information.

PROJECT 21	Terry Battery Cable Upgrade

Tools Needed: 10-mm wrench; 12-mm, ½-inch or ⁹⁄₁₆-inch wrench; various sockets for battery tray removal if necessary

Time: 30 minutes to an hour   **Talent:** Intermediate   **Cost:** $40

Parts required: Terry battery cable kit

Performance Gain: You'll have more cranking power with less voltage loss.

I recommend upgrading the battery cables on your bike to a much more capable cable for flexing and handling increased power. A company called Terry makes super-flexible battery cables made up of 1,650 strands of wire, as opposed to the stock cable of 180 strands. Upgrading to these cables will give you more cranking power with less voltage loss than stock cables. The smaller wires make the cables much more flexible and able to deliver more current. You can order these cables, designed for specific bikes, as part of a kit or individually.

To change the battery cables, you'll need to first remove the battery from the bike. On my 1996 XL that meant starting with the seat and taking all the battery covers off. Depending on the bike you're working with, this upgrade may involve removing parts and covers to get to the battery. I also had to take the battery tray off the bike for better access to the cables. Remember, when disconnecting the battery disconnect the negative cable first and the positive cable last.

This is basically a straightforward job. Disconnect your stock cables and replace them with the new ones. This particular job turned into a bit more of a hassle because of a bolt that didn't want to budge. I asked R.T. to give me a hand and he took some PB Blaster (penetrating oil) and soaked the bolt and worked it free.

I ordered the Terry cable kit for my bike's year and model but the negative cable terminal was not big enough to fit over the ³⁄₈-inch bolt. I didn't want to force it for fear of weakening the terminal, so we took a die grinder to ream the hole out a little more to slip over the bolt.

The last step is to route your cables back to the battery tray, reinstall the battery tray and battery, and finally connect the new cables up. Remember, always connect positive first and negative last. Now this bike is set up with battery cables that I'll never have to worry about breaking or losing power. Gaining the cranking power is a great thing too, especially with engine upgrades.

For this XL battery cable upgrade, the battery box covers need to be removed. Keep track of parts when removing them so you don't waste time hunting them down when it's time to reinstall.

The battery tray should be removed next in order to get proper clearance to the cables. Keep your bolts in order. This will help the job go a little faster.

Above: This battery cable kit was listed for this specific model, but once I got into the project the terminal on the negative cable was not large enough to fit over the ⅜-inch bolt. I had to use a die grinder to ream out the bolt hole on the terminal to fit over the ⅜-inch bolt. This is not my favorite thing to do because it can weaken the terminal. Left: Ah, one of those infamous stubborn bolts I talked about. I grabbed R.T. from his project and had him work this bolt loose for me. He used some "PB" (Penetrating Blaster oil) and kept working the bolt until it was freed.

Upgrade parts are usually noticeably different than the stock parts they are replacing. You can see how much more flexible the Terry battery cable is next to the stock battery cables.

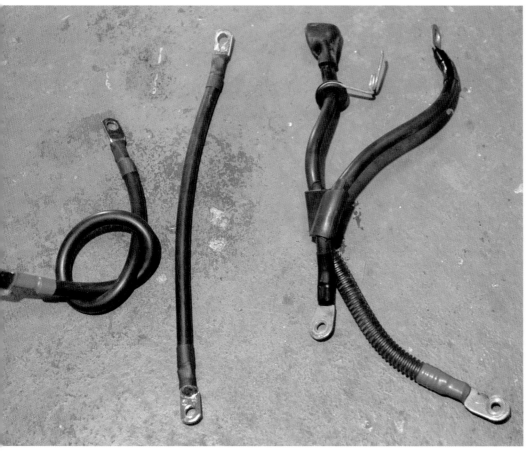

Always use Loctite on any bolt that requires it. A small amount goes a long way, so don't be over-generous with it. Your service manual will point out which bolts will need Loctite and which strength to use.

Left: Here you can see the Terry battery cables on the bike. Notice how flexible they are just hanging. No need to worry about breakage with these super-flexible wires.

Important! When reinstalling the battery on the bike, reconnect the positive cable first and the negative cable last.

INSPECTING LIGHTING AND YOUR HORN

Once I realized how important it was for me to be inspecting my bike and paying attention to what it was telling me, I made up a little routine of things to look at before I get on my bike for a ride.

Check over your lighting. You want to make sure your turn signals, brake lights, and headlights are all working before you start interacting with traffic. Check all your lighting to make sure it's all good. If you have a burned-out bulb, your owner's and service manuals will have a part number listed for replacement. Change any bulbs that are burned out.

You may find that your brake light is not working but your bulb is good. The next place to check is the brake switches.

The front brake switch is in the handlebar controls and the rear is wired into the rear brake line. Eliminate which is not working and replace the switch. The part number for your model will be listed in your parts book. If you don't have a parts book, the salesperson at the parts counter can hook you up if you have your model and year handy.

If you have a horn on your bike, you might as well take advantage of it and make sure it's working. I usually only use my horn if I see one of those cars creeping out of a driveway that may not see me. I'll blast the horn to give them a heads-up that I'm out there. The horn works well for that. It takes just a few seconds to make sure all the lighting on your bike is working properly, so be sure to take the time to do it.

You'll want to make sure your brake light is working by performing routine lighting inspections. Be sure to test both front and rear.

During lighting inspections, cup your hand over the lens so that you can see if your light works and your turn signals are operating correctly.

Bulb replacement is pretty straightforward. You'll find the bulb's part number listed in your service manual.

ELECTRICAL 101

WIRING

Believe it or not, there are quite a few wires on a motorcycle. Just look at the wiring diagram in your shop manual. Yeah, it's very intimidating, and even after dealing with bike wiring for six years now it still scares the hell out of me. Your mysterious wiring scheme will short out on you and the problem area is often hidden somewhere.

If you're having a wiring issue somewhere in your main harness (inside the frame or between the single-sided gas tanks), it's best to let a shop or certified mechanic deal with it.

There will be times an exposed wire or one easily accessible wire decides to break, or something wore through the insulation and it's grounding itself out. If you have never reconnected a wire before, it's really not that bad. You'll want to swing by Radio Shack and get yourself a soldering gun, solder, some flux, and an assortment of shrink tubes

in different sizes. You'll also want a set of wire pliers or wire cutters.

Go ahead and cut the wire at the damaged area. I hope you'll have enough wire to reconnect without needing an extra length of wire. If you need to add a length, cut a little piece of the wire and bring it to a shop or dealership and ask the parts guy for a length of that gauge of wire in whatever length you need. You should also be able to get wire at Radio Shack.

Use the pliers to strip the wire bare on both sides and prepare a length of shrink tube long enough to cover your connection. Place the shrink tube away from the connection. Twist the two pieces snugly around each other, dab some flux on them, and use the soldering gun to fuse the two pieces together. Once you have good fusion, pull the shrink tube down to cover the connection you just made and use a heat gun or a hair dryer to shrink the tube snug

150

around your connection. Don't hold the heat in one spot for too long or you'll burn through the shrink tube and you'll be throwing that soldering gun around instead of a wrench!

Let me tell you, this service work I'm talking about is not hard at all. Don't ever feel that you can't do the work. Once you gain the knowledge, you won't have it any other way. I would never leave the fate of my bike to someone else. Of course, if the job was out of my means, like rebuilding a transmission, then I would get some help from someone I trust. But this basic service maintenance work is a piece of cake.

I have friends who are stunt trick riders. They ride their bikes on a 90-degree wooden wall, the American Motor Drome (otherwise known as the Wall of Death). Now you can imagine these guys and girls need their bikes to be in top shape. Do you think they leave the fate of their bike up to someone else? Nope. They all maintain and know first-hand the working condition of their bikes. They have to; their lives depend on their bike's running condition.

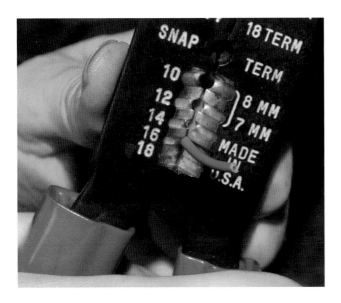

Above left: Have a good set of wire strippers and crimpers on hand, and strip the wire clean of the insulation. Above right: Cut a length of shrink tube long enough to cover the connection, and slide it on one side of the wire just below the connection.

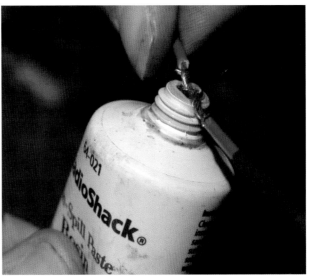

Above left: Twist the two pieces of bare wire together. Try to make the connection tight and uniform. Above right: Apply a little flux on the bare wire connection so the solder will stick.

Heat up the wire with the solder gun so it's hot enough to melt the flux and fuse the solder to your connection.

Don't let the strange technical words like "primary chain" or "torque spec" scare you away. You'll become familiar with them and they will roll off your tongue in no time. I honestly believe everyone who rides, man or woman, needs to be familiar with their bike.

The best way to become one with your bike is to maintain it and read everything it's telling you. If your brake pads are getting low, you're going to ride your bike differently if you're aware of it. If your tires are getting to the point of needing to be changed, you're going to ride your bike differently. Knowing the working condition of your bike will make you a smarter rider. Smarter in the sense that you will be handling any situation you're in with the proper knowledge.

There's a reason it's called preventative maintenance. In the long run, you are looking out for yourself and ensuring a safe ride. I keep telling people that the bike is an extension of their body. Pay attention to your bike just like you do your body. If not for the satisfaction of doing it yourself, then for the safety of a well-maintained machine. You will feel more confident riding your motorcycle.

Slide the shrink tube up over the connection and heat with a heat gun. A lighter will also work just fine, as long as you're not working near any flammable liquids or gasses. Don't leave the heat in one spot for too long or you might burn through the shrink tube.

CHAPTER 6
SIMPLE ROADSIDE REPAIRS AND TRAVEL TOOLKITS

"EVERY RIDE" CHECKLIST

This is a little routine habit I've developed before every ride, and I hope you'll get yourself in the habit as well. A few short minutes can ensure you a safe and confident ride:

- Tire inspection
- Air pressure check
- Brake pad check
- Headlight, brake light, and turn signals
- Throttle response
- Clutch cable adjustment
- Horn

I hope you'll never find yourself on the side of the road, but mechanical things always have the potential for failure. Everything discussed in earlier chapters is to help keep you from being on the side of the road, but like the Boy Scouts, we need to be prepared.

Virtually every motorcyclist will find himself or herself making a simple repair on the side of the road. Let's put together a travel toolkit.

If you have saddlebags, you can simply throw this toolkit in one of the bags. If you don't have saddlebags, you can always buy a tool pouch to keep on your front forks or a tank bag. These are also great for a cell phone, extra set of glasses, maybe night-time clear or yellow glasses, and anything else you want to have handy.

Since it is the twenty-first century, we'll go ahead and endorse the marvels of modern times and take advantage of the cell phone. Honestly, let's face it, if you find yourself stranded on the side of the road alone there is no better tool to have.

As for traditional tools, here's a list:

- Spark-plug wrench and a spare set of spark plugs
- Screwdriver (to fit your air cleaner cover)
- A travel-sized ratchet and socket set with the most common sizes on your bike
- Allen key kit and torx bit kits with the most common sizes you'll need

CruzTOOLS travel tool kits are your best bet for roadside repairs. This outbacker tool (above) is so small it will even fit in your jacket pocket.

Right: CruzTOOLS did their homework and compiled a travel tool pack containing every tool you could need and customized for every model. With a lifetime guarantee, you know you can count on these tools to perform when you need them to.

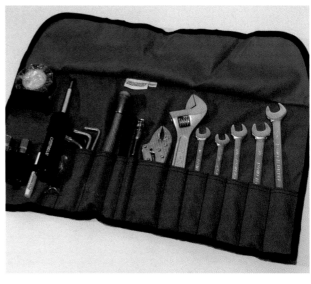

A roll of electrical tape on your bike for quick and temporary wire connection repairs

Last, but very important, a wrench to fit your battery terminals should you need to make any electrical repairs

Now, if you're digging around in your garage to put together a toolkit you may risk the chance of forgetting the one tool you would need if something were to happen. CruzTOOLs makes some really neat toolkits to travel with. But make sure it contains all the tools in all the sizes you'll need.

Having a dedicated toolkit on your bike is much easier than trying to round up tools separately. It's also nice to keep your garage tools separate to lower the chances of losing any of them.

Let's face it, the time you find yourself on the side of the road is usually at night, it's starting to rain, you're in the middle of nowhere, and it's just the worst possible time for a breakdown. Your kit should have everything from that most-important 10-mm battery wrench to a flashlight and tire gauge. It's really important to be using a toolkit you can depend on. This takes us back to what I mentioned earlier about buying tools from a reputable tool company, and CruzTOOLS' kits come with a lifetime guarantee. So you know you can rely on these tools to perform when you need them to.

SIMPLE ROADSIDE REPAIRS AND TROUBLESHOOTING

I won't be able to cover everything that could possibly go wrong with your bike; but if anything you read here does happen, I hope reading this will get you out of a jam. Of course, if anything more than just a quick fix is in order you'll want to get your bike to a repair shop as soon as you can.

If your bike starts coughing on you and feeling sluggish, try changing the plugs. You'd be surprised how a fresh set of plugs will improve your engine. Don't forget to gap them before you pack them in your toolkit.

If your bike starts running rough, I'd recommend pulling over somewhere to pull the air cleaner cover off and take a look at the air filter. If you've been doing the service maintenance at regular intervals, a dirty air filter shouldn't be troubling you. But if you skipped looking at it, now's the time.

If you don't have a fuel gauge and you can't calculate your fuel mileage, sometimes you might find yourself on the side of the road because you're out of gas. I hope you're riding with a friend so you can rob some fuel from your buddy's bike. Try finding an empty container somewhere or, if you have saddlebags, keep a bottle of water on hand so you can empty the bottle and use that. Disconnect the fuel line from your friend's bike and steal enough to get you to the nearest gas station. Hey, what are friends for, right?

When you find yourself on the side of the road, having the right tools means everything.

Recycle your used oil into empty oil bottles or any storage containers you have. You need to properly dispose of the used oil. You can find listings in the phone book for companies that will remove the oil for you or allow you to drop it off.

Flat tires—they suck, what can more can I say? Lots of times the problem is from riding over a nail or screw, but if you're inspecting your bike before you leave, maybe you'd find the culprit and take care of the problem before you left for that ride. If you run over a nail or a screw while you're out riding and the tire does go flat, having a can of "fix-a-flat" (for tubeless only) will get you somewhere safe. Remember, fix-a-flat doesn't give you a free ticket to keep riding all day. Get that bike somewhere and have the tire changed immediately.

If you have tires that run tubes, usually with wire wheels, then just call someone to pick you up. Fix-a-flat will not work on tube tires.

Honestly, most of the electronic ignition bikes today don't really leave you on the side of the road as often as the "point-and-condenser" styles used to. There just isn't that much room for error anymore. If you are riding a bike with a point-and-condenser ignition setup and the bike is misfiring and coughing, a new set of points will more than likely clear that out for you.

Everything this book has discussed and walked you through is for preventative maintenance, to try to keep you from being on the side of the road. The proper maintenance of your bike is meant to keep you riding and enjoying the time out on the road. Unfortunately, human and mechanical error often work together in perfect harmony, and you'll find yourself in a pinch no matter how diligent you've been.

PROPER DISCARDING OF OLD FLUIDS, BATTERIES, ETC.

Every state is different and each county, town, and city will have its own set of rules for environmental waste concerns. One thing I know is that every state has made it illegal to dump oil on the ground or in a lake, stream, river, etc., due to the effect it would have on the wildlife and public water systems. I'm sure you're already aware of that and wouldn't even consider it. It's common sense.

Look in your phone book for oil removal companies; they will be more than happy to take your old oil for you. Sometimes you'll find gas stations or other businesses that will take used oil for heating purposes. Some companies use oil heaters, and by taking your unwanted used oil they are getting fuel for their heating systems. Oil change chains, like Jiffy Lube or Valvoline, will often discard used oil for you as well.

You can store and transport the old oil in the bottles the fresh oil came in, just take the funnel and stick it in the old bottles and fill them up from your drain pan. Coffee cans also work great and are a little easier to fill up.

Fogging oil and fuel stabilizer help maintain your bike when stored for a long period of time, such as during the winter months.

When it's time to bring your bike out of storage, give it a full inspection. Your service manual has a check list for this.

When buying a new battery for your bike, ask if the shop you're purchasing from can discard your old battery for you. You should never throw your battery in the trash.

Tires are also treated as a dangerous material and should be disposed of properly. Look in the phone book for a tire removal company or find a business that will take them off your hands and properly dispose of them. Usually the shop you have change your tires will discard the old tires for you and charge a nominal fee for that service; this is well worth the money and is that much less for you to deal with.

Properly discarding of these items is the last step in maintaining your bike. It's your responsibility to maintain your bike from start to finish.

PROPER STORAGE OF YOUR BIKE

Depending on where you live, you might have to store your bike during winter months. If so, there are several things you should be doing to care for your bike properly. When storing the bike, you will want to have the fuel tank full and add a fuel stabilizer. Make sure the petcock (fuel valve) is turned to the off position.

It's best to drain all gas from the carburetor. You can have your local shop do this work for you if you don't feel confident. You can also drain all gas from the fuel tank and spray the inside with a rust preventative. I opt for the first option as it's much easier to handle.

Check the tire air pressure and, if storing the bike for a long period, prop the bike up on a lift or stand so no pressure is on the tires. If that's not possible, you should move the bike back and forth on a regular basis during storage to prevent the tires from getting soft spots from resting too long in one place.

When storing the bike for several months, you can also pull the spark plugs and spray a fogging oil into the cylinders to prevent them from rusting.

You should remove the battery from the bike and connect your battery tender.

When it's time to bring your bike back out of storage, it's a good idea to put your bike into first gear, disengage the clutch, and push the bike back and forth a few times. This will ensure the clutch is working properly and you won't have to worry about the bike moving at initial start-up.

When it's time to ride again, make sure your battery is fully charged and place it back in the bike. Remove and inspect spark plugs and change them if needed. Clean out your air filter. Check all your fluid levels and fill them if needed.

Start the engine and let it reach normal running temperature. Time to enjoy all that hard work you put into servicing your bike and ride! The freedom of wrenching your own bike will take your rides to the next level.

SOURCES

Bel-Ray (oils)
P.O. Box 526
Farmingdale, NJ 07727
732.295.7113
www.belray.com

Terry Components (battery cables)
2916 E. 4th Ave.
Spearfish, SD 57783
866.388.3779
www.terrycomp.com

CruzTOOLS
P.O. Box 250
Standard, CA 95373-0250
888.909.8665
www.cruztools.com

Performance Machine
6892 Marlin Circle
LaPalma, CA 90623
800.479.4037
www.performancemachine.com

Ferodo U.S.A (brakes)
4200 Diplomacy Way
Ft. Worth, TX 76155
866.337.6361
www.ferodousa.com

Custom Chrome
16100 Jacqueline Ct.
Morgan Hill, CA 95037
800.359.5700
www.customchrome.com

Drag Specialties
P.O. Box 5222
Janesville, WI 53547-5222
800.369.1000
www.dragspecialties.com

T.P. Engineering
5 Francis J. Clarke Circle
Bethel, CT 06801
866.873.6446
www.tpeng.com

Tech Cycle Performance Products
Inc. (starters)
55 Humeville Ave.
Penndel, PA 19047
215.702.1482
www.techcycle.com

Mikuni (carburetors)
8910 Mikuni Ave.
Northbridge, CA 91324-3496
818.885.1242
www.mikuni.com

Clymer Repair Manuals
9800 Metcalf Ave.
Overland Park, KS 66212
800.262.1954

Harley-Davidson Motor Co.
3700 W. Juneau Ave.
Milwaukee, WI 53208
414.342.4680
www.harley-davidson.com

Interstate Battery
1700 Dixon St.
Des Moines, IA 50316
888.772.3600
www.interstatebatteries.com

Deltran Corp. (Battery tender)
801 U.S. Hwy 92E
Deland, FL 32724
877.456.7901
www.batterytender.com

S&S Cycle Inc.
14025 County Hwy. G
Viola, WI 54664
866.244.2673
www.sscycle.com

Sears Craftsman
www.sears.com

Snap-on Tools
877.762.7664
www.snapon.com

JIMS Tools
555 Dawson Dr.
Camarillo, CA 93012
805.482.6913
www.jimsusa.com

Dunlop Tire Corp.
P.O. Box 1109
Buffalo, NY 14240-1109
800.548.4714
www.dunloptire.com

Metzeler Motorcycle Tires
100 Pirelli Dr.
Rome, GA 30161-3538
706.368.5826
www.us.metzelermoto.com

Wizards-RJ Star Inc. (cleaning products)
11469 8th St. NE
Hanover, MN 55341
800.356.7223
www.wizardsproducts.com

Avon Tyres
407 Howell Ave.
Edmonds, WA 98020
800.624.7470
www.avonmotorcycle.com

Michelin Tire Corp.
1 Parkway St.
Greenville, SC 29615
888.716.5888
www.michelin.com

Continental Tire
41 Strong St.
Wallington, NJ 07057
614.855.6960
www.conti-online.com

Goodridge U.S.A. Inc. (brake lines)
529 Van Ness Ave.
Torrance, CA 90501
800.662.2466
www.goodridge.net

SBS brakes
3501 Kennedy Rd.
P.O. Box 5222
Janesville, WI 53547-5222
608.758.1111

EBC (brakes)
13010 Bradley Ave.
Sylmar, CA 91342
818.362.5534
www.ebcbrakes.com

Vanson Leathers
951 Broadway
Fall River, MA 02724
508.678.2000
www.vansonleathers.com

Supertapp Industries Inc. (exhaust)
4540 W. 160th St.
Cleveland, OH 44135
216.265.8400
www.supertrapp.com

INDEX

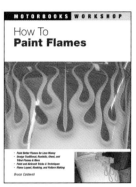